Essential Questionnaires For Child Listings

NAVIGATING

SOCIAL SECURITY DISABILITY

A Guide To Disability Law

A Kelly Neal, Esq.
Neal Student Support Advocacy & Disability, LLC

COPYRIGHT PAGE

 Published by Neal Student Support Advocacy & Disability, LLC; Macon, Georgia

Library of Congress No: 2025923351

ISBN No: 979-8-9929441-5-0
Cover design by A. Kelly Neal, Esq.
Printed in the United States of America
For more information, visit www.SSAdisability.org

Disclaimer:
This book is intended for informational and educational purposes only. It does not constitute legal advice or establish an attorney-client relationship. Readers should consult a qualified attorney for legal guidance regarding specific situations. While every effort has been made to ensure accuracy, the author and publisher assume no responsibility for errors or omissions.

The information contained in this book is provided for informational purposes only, and should not be construed as legal advice on any subject matter. This book is similarly not intended as a solicitation for or advertisement of A. Kelly Neal, Esq.'s legal services. Transmission of the information contained in this book is not intended to create, and receipt does not constitute, an attorney-client or business relationship between the sender and receiver. An attorney-client relationship between A. Kelly Neal, Esq. and any reader of this book does not exist unless and until an agreement has been reached between you and A. Kelly Neal, Esq. to handle a particular matter. Receipt of unsolicited confidential information by A. Kelly Neal, Esq. will not disqualify the firm from representing another party in any matter to which the information relates. Laws differ by jurisdiction, and the information in this book may not apply to every reader. No recipients of content from this book should act or refrain from acting on the basis of any content included in the book without seeking the appropriate legal or other professional advice on the particular facts and circumstances at issue from an attorney licensed in the recipient's state. A. Kelly Neal, Esq. expressly disclaims all liability in respect to actions taken or not taken based on any or all the contents of this book. A. Kelly Neal, Esq. is licensed to practice law only in the State of Georgia.

Law is constantly evolving. The information in this book is intended for general informational purposes and may not reflect the most current legal developments. This book provides an overview of the subject matter covered and is sold with the understanding that neither the publisher nor the author is providing legal or other professional services. For legal advice regarding a specific situation, you should consult a qualified attorney.

DEDICATION

To the resilient individuals navigating the challenges of disability—your strength, perseverance, and dignity inspire this work. And to the advocates, caregivers, and professionals who stand beside them—may this guide empower your continued fight for justice and access.

With deepest respect,
A. Kelly Neal, Esq

ACKNOWLEDGMENTS

To everyone who contributed to this book, thank you from the bottom of my heart. Your support, insights, and efforts have been invaluable, and I am deeply grateful. Your contributions have not gone unnoticed—they have made this book possible, and I appreciate each and every one of you.

TABLE OF CONTENTS

SSA-100.04-LOW BIRTH WEIGHT IN INFANTS

Patient Name:_______________________________ Date of Exam:____________

What was the infant's birth weight (grams)?

- ☐ Less than 1200 grams
- ☐ 1200 grams or more

Please provide the gestational age at birth and corresponding birth weight:

Gestational Age (weeks)	Birth Weight (grams)	Meets Criteria?
37–40	☐ 2000 grams or less	☐ Yes ☐ No
36	☐ 1875 grams or less	☐ Yes ☐ No
35	☐ 1700 grams or less	☐ Yes ☐ No
34	☐ 1500 grams or less	☐ Yes ☐ No
33	☐ 1325 grams or less	☐ Yes ☐ No
32	☐ 1250 grams or less	☐ Yes ☐ No

Gestational age of the infant at birth (weeks): ______________________________

Birth weight (grams): ______________________________

Date of birth: ______________________________

Physician Signature: ____________________ Physician Name: ____________________

SSA-100.05-FAILURE TO THRIVE IN CHILDREN

Patient Name:______________________________________ Date of Exam:_____________

For children from birth to attainment of age 2
Are there three weight-for-length measurements that meet all the following criteria?

☐ Yes ☐ No

☐ Taken within a consecutive 12-month period ☐ At least 60 days apart.

☐ Less than the third percentile on the weight-for-length table under 105.08B1.

For children age 2 to attainment of age 3
Are there three BMI-for-age measurements that meet all the following criteria?

☐ Yes ☐ No

☐ Taken within a consecutive 12-month period ☐ At least 60 days apart.

☐ Less than the third percentile on the BMI-for-age table under 105.08B2.

Is there a standardized developmental assessment (see 100.00C3b) documenting:
Development not more than two-thirds of the level typically expected for the child's age?

☐ Yes ☐ No

A valid score at least two standard deviations below the mean?

☐ Yes ☐ No

Are there two narrative developmental reports (see 100.00C3c) that:
Are dated at least 120 days apart?

☐ Yes ☐ No

Indicate current development not more than two-thirds of the level typically expected for the child's age?

☐ Yes ☐ No

Child's age: ______________________
Date(s) of weight-for-length or BMI-for-age measurements:

(a)____________________(b)____________________(c)____________________
Date(s) of developmental assessment(s) or narrative report(s):

(a)____________________(b)____________________(c)____________________

Physician Signature: _______________________ Physician Name: ______________________

SSA-101.15-DISORDERS OF THE SKELETAL SPINE RESULTING IN COMPROMISE OF A NERVE ROOT

Patient Name:____ Date of Exam:______________

Neuro-anatomic (radicular) distribution of symptoms consistent with compromise of the affected nerve root(s): ☐ Pain ☐ Paresthesia ☐ Muscle fatigue

Radicular distribution of neurological signs present during physical examination or diagnostic testing, evidenced by:

☐ 1. Muscle weakness

☐ 2. Sign(s) of nerve root irritation, tension, or compression, consistent with compromise of the affected nerve root

☐ 3. Sensory changes evidenced by:

- ☐ a. Decreased sensation
- ☐ b. Sensory nerve deficit (abnormal sensory nerve latency) on electrodiagnostic testing

☐ 4. Decreased deep tendon reflexes

Findings on imaging consistent with compromise of a nerve root(s) in the cervical or lumbosacral spine: ☐ Yes ☐ No

Impairment-related physical limitation of musculoskeletal functioning that has lasted, or is expected to last, for a continuous period of at least 12 months, with medical documentation of at least one of the following:

☐ 1. A documented medical need for:

- ☐ Walker ☐ Bilateral canes ☐ Bilateral crutches
- ☐ Wheeled and seated mobility device involving the use of both hands

☐ 2. An inability to use one upper extremity to independently initiate, sustain, and complete age-appropriate activities involving fine and gross movements, with a documented medical need for:

- ☐ One-handed, hand-held assistive device requiring use of the other upper extremity
- ☐ Wheeled and seated mobility device involving the use of one hand

☐ 3. An inability to use both upper extremities to the extent that neither can be used to independently initiate, sustain, and complete age-appropriate activities involving fine and gross movements

Physician Signature: __________________________ Physician Name: _________________________

SSA-101.16-LUMBAR SPINAL STENOSIS RESULTING IN COMPROMISE OF THE CAUDA EQUINA

Patient Name:_______________________________________ Date of Exam:____________

Does the patient exhibit any of the following symptoms? (Check all that apply)

☐ Nonradicular distribution of pain in one or both lower extremities

☐ Nonradicular distribution of sensory loss in one or both lower extremities

☐ Neurogenic claudication

Does the patient exhibit any of the following signs during physical examination or on diagnostic testing? (Check all that apply)

1. Muscle Weakness [ ]-Yes [ ]-No

2. Sensory Changes (At least one must be checked if this category is applicable)

☐ Decreased sensation

☐ Sensory nerve deficit (abnormal sensory nerve latency) on electrodiagnostic testing

☐ Areflexia, trophic ulceration, or bladder or bowel incontinence

3. Decreased Deep Tendon Reflexes in One or Both Lower Extremities

[ ]-Yes [ ]-No

Do imaging studies (MRI, CT, X-ray) or an operative report show findings consistent with compromise of the cauda equina with lumbar spinal stenosis?

[ ]-Yes [ ]-No

Has the impairment lasted, or is it expected to last, for a continuous period of at least 12 months?

[ ]-Yes [ ]-No

If Yes, does the patient have at least one of the following documented medical needs? (Check all that apply)

☐ A walker, bilateral canes, bilateral crutches, or a wheeled and seated mobility device involving the use of both hands

☐ An inability to use one upper extremity to independently initiate, sustain, and complete age-appropriate activities involving fine and gross movements, and a documented medical need for:

☐ A one-handed, hand-held assistive device requiring use of the other upper extremity

☐ A wheeled and seated mobility device involving the use of one hand

Physician Signature: _________________________ Physician Name: ________________________

SSA-101.17-RECONSTRUCTIVE SURGERY OR SURGICAL ARTHRODESIS OF A MAJOR WEIGHT BEARING JOINT

Patient Name:_______________________________________ Date of Exam:______________

Has the patient undergone reconstructive surgery or surgical arthrodesis of a major weight-bearing joint? ☐-Yes ☐-No

If yes, provide the date and type of surgery:

____

Specify the joint affected:

☐ Hip ☐ Knee ☐ Ankle ☐ Other: ______________________________

Does the patient have an impairment-related physical limitation of musculoskeletal functioning that has lasted or is expected to last for a continuous period of at least 12 months?

☐-Yes ☐-No

If yes, describe the functional limitations:

____

Does the patient have a documented medical need for any of the following? (Check all that apply)

☐ Walker ☐ Bilateral canes ☐ Bilateral crutches

☐ Wheeled and seated mobility device involving the use of both hands

Additional Comments:

____

____

Physician's Name: ______________________ Physician's Signature: ______________________

SSA-101.18-ABNORMALITY OF A MAJOR JOINT(S) IN ANY EXTREMITY

Patient Name:____ Date of Exam:______________

Diagnosis: ____

Affected Joint(s): ____

Does the patient experience chronic joint pain or stiffness? ☐ Yes ☐ No
If yes, please describe:____

____

Does the patient exhibit abnormal motion, instability, or immobility of the affected joint(s)?
☐ Yes ☐ No
If yes, please describe:____

____

Does the patient exhibit any of the following on physical examination? (Check all that apply)
☐ Subluxation ☐ Contracture ☐ Bony or fibrous ankylosis
☐ Other (please specify): ____

Does imaging reveal any of the following abnormalities? (Check all that apply)
☐ Joint space narrowing ☐ Bony destruction ☐ Ankylosis or arthrodesis
☐ Other (please specify): ____

Has the impairment lasted, or is it expected to last, for at least 12 months?☐ Yes ☐ No

Does the patient have medical documentation of at least one of the following? (Check all that apply)

☐ A documented medical need for a walker, bilateral canes, bilateral crutches, or a wheeled and seated mobility device requiring the use of both hands.

☐ An inability to use one upper extremity to independently initiate, sustain, and complete age-appropriate activities involving fine and gross movements, AND a documented medical need for a one-handed, hand-held assistive device that requires use of the other upper extremity or a wheeled and seated mobility device requiring one hand.

☐ An inability to use both upper extremities to the extent that neither can be used to independently initiate, sustain, and complete age-appropriate activities involving fine and gross movements.

Additional Comments:____

Physician's Name: ________________________Physician's Signature: ________________________

SSA-101.19-PATHOLOGIC FRACTURES & MUSCULOSKELETAL IMPAIRMENTS

Patient Name:_______________________________________ Date of Exam:_____________

Diagnosis: ____

Has the patient experienced pathologic fractures on at least three separate occasions within a 12-month period? ☐ Yes ☐ No

If yes, please provide details of each occurrence, including dates and affected bones:

____

Has the patient's musculoskeletal impairment lasted or is it expected to last for a continuous period of at least 12 months? ☐ Yes ☐ No

Please indicate the applicable functional limitations (check all that apply):

Documented Medical Need for Assistive Devices

☐ Walker ☐ Bilateral canes ☐ Bilateral crutches

☐ Wheeled and seated mobility device requiring use of both hands

Inability to Use One Upper Extremity for Fine and Gross Movements

☐ Yes, and requires a one-handed, hand-held assistive device requiring the use of the other upper extremity

☐ Yes, and requires a wheeled and seated mobility device involving the use of one hand

Inability to Use Both Upper Extremities

☐ Yes, unable to independently initiate, sustain, and complete age-appropriate activities involving fine and gross movements

Additional Comments:____

____

Physician's Name: ______________________Physician's Signature: ______________________

SSA-101.20-AMPUTATION DUE TO ANY CAUSE

Patient Name:_____________________________________ Date of Exam:_____________

Amputation due to any cause (see 101.00K), documented by A, B, C, or D:A. Amputation of both upper extremities at any level at or above the wrists (carpal joints), up to and including the shoulder (glenohumeral) joint.

[] Yes [] No

Hemipelvectomy or hip disarticulation

[] Yes [] No

Amputation of one upper extremity at or above the wrist (carpal joints) and amputation of one lower extremity at or above the ankle (talocrural joint), with medical documentation of at least one of the following:

[] 1. Documented medical need for a walker, bilateral canes, or bilateral crutches, or a wheeled and seated mobility device involving the use of both hands.

[] 2. Documented medical need for a one-handed, hand-held assistive device requiring the use of the other upper extremity or a wheeled and seated mobility device involving the use of one hand.

[ ] 3. Inability to use the remaining upper extremity to independently initiate, sustain, and complete age-appropriate activities involving fine and gross movements.

[] None of the above.

Amputation of one or both lower extremities at or above the ankle (talocrural joint), with complications of the residual limb(s) that have lasted, or are expected to last, for a continuous period of at least 12 months, and medical documentation of both of the following:

[] 1. Inability to use a prosthesis(es).

[] 2. Documented medical need for a walker, bilateral canes, or bilateral crutches, or a wheeled and seated mobility device involving the use of both hands.

[] None of the above.

Additional Comments:____

____

Physician's Name: ______________________Physician's Signature: ______________________

SSA-101.21-SOFT TISSUE INJURY OR ABNORMALITY UNDER CONTINUING SURGICAL MANAGEMENT

Patient Name:____ Date of Exam:______________

Does the patient have documented evidence of continuing surgical management directed toward saving, reconstructing, or replacing the affected body part?

☐ Yes ☐ No

If yes, please describe the surgical management:

____

____

____

Has the surgical management been ongoing, or is it expected to be ongoing, for a continuous period of at least 12 months?

☐ Yes ☐ No

If yes, provide the start date and expected duration:

Start Date: __________________ Expected Duration: __________________________________

Has the patient achieved maximum benefit from therapy?

☐ Yes ☐ No

If no, please describe the ongoing therapeutic interventions and why maximum benefit has not yet been achieved:

____

____

____

Physician's Name: ________________________Physician's Signature: _______________________

SSA-101.22-NON-HEALING OR COMPLEX FRACTURE OF THE FEMUR, TIBIA, PELVIS, OR TALOCRURAL BONES

Patient Name:_______________________________________ Date of Exam:_____________

Has the patient been diagnosed with a non-healing or complex fracture of the femur, tibia, pelvis, or one or more talocrural bones?

☐ Yes ☐ No

If yes, specify the affected bone(s): ____

Is there imaging evidence that a solid union has not formed? (e.g., X-ray, CT, MRI findings)

☐ Yes ☐ No

Date of most recent imaging: ____

Imaging findings: ____

Is the fracture clinically assessed as not solid?

☐ Yes ☐ No

Has the patient's musculoskeletal functioning been impaired due to the fracture?

☐ Yes ☐ No

Has this impairment lasted, or is it expected to last, for at least 12 continuous months?

☐ Yes ☐ No

Describe the functional limitations resulting from this impairment:

____

____

Does the patient require any of the following mobility aids due to the impairment? *(Check all that apply)*

☐ Walker ☐ Bilateral canes ☐ Bilateral crutches

☐ Wheeled and seated mobility device involving the use of both hands

Is the medical need for the above device(s) documented in the patient's records?

☐ Yes ☐ No

Please provide additional clinical observations regarding the patient's mobility limitations and medical need for assistive devices:

____

Physician's Name: _______________________Physician's Signature: _______________________

SSA-101.23-NON-HEALING OR COMPLEX FRACTURE OF AN UPPER EXTREMITY

Patient Name:____ Date of Exam:______________

Diagnosis:____

Has the patient been diagnosed with a nonunion or complex fracture of the shaft of the humerus, radius, or ulna? ☐ Yes ☐ No

Date of initial diagnosis: ____

Imaging or diagnostic studies confirming the condition:

☐ X-ray ☐ MRI ☐ CT scan ☐ Other (please specify):____________________

Is the patient under continuing surgical management directed toward the restoration of functional use of the affected extremity? ☐ Yes ☐ No

Type(s) of surgical interventions performed: ______________________________________

Date(s) of surgical procedures: ____

Is additional surgical intervention planned? ☐ Yes ☐ No

If yes, expected procedure and date: ______________________________________

Does the patient have medical documentation of an inability to independently initiate, sustain, and complete age-appropriate activities involving fine and gross motor movements?

☐ Yes ☐ No

Describe specific limitations (e.g., difficulty grasping, lifting, reaching, writing, dressing, feeding, etc.):

____

____

Have these limitations lasted, or are they expected to last, for a continuous period of at least 12 months? ☐ Yes ☐ No

Date of onset of functional limitations: ______________________________________

Additional Comments:

____

____

Physician's Name: ________________________Physician's Signature: ________________________

SSA-101.24-MUSCULOSKELETAL DISORDERS OF INFANTS AND TODDLERS (BIRTH TO AGE 3) WITH DEVELOPMENTAL MOTOR DELAY

Patient Name:_______________________________ Date of Exam:__________

Has the child undergone a standardized developmental motor assessment?

☐ Yes ☐ No

If yes, please complete the following:

Name of the assessment tool used: ______________________________

Date of assessment: ______________________________

Results:

Does the assessment indicate motor development at no more than one-half of the level typically expected for the child's age? ☐ Yes ☐ No

Does the assessment provide a valid score that is at least three standard deviations below the mean? ☐ Yes ☐ No

Have you provided or reviewed two narrative developmental reports documenting motor development? ☐ Yes ☐ No

If yes, please provide details:

Date of first report: ______________________________

Findings: ______________________________

Does the report indicate motor development at no more than one-half of the level typically expected for the child's age? ☐ Yes ☐ No

Date of second report (at least 120 days apart from the first): ______________________________

Findings: ______________________________

Does the report indicate motor development at no more than one-half of the level typically expected for the child's age? ☐ Yes ☐ No

Please attach copies of both reports if available.

Additional Comments:

____

____

Physician's Name: __________________ Physician's Signature: __________________

SSA-102.02-LOSS OF CENTRAL VISUAL ACUITY

Patient Name:_______________________________________ Date of Exam:_____________

Diagnosis: ____

Remaining vision in the better eye after best correction is 20/200 or less

[ ] Yes [ ] No

OR

The patient is unable to participate in visual acuity testing using Snellen methodology or other comparable testing, with clinical findings that fixation and visual-following behavior are absent in the better eye, and one of the following (check all that apply):

[ ] Abnormal anatomical findings indicating a visual acuity of 20/200 or less in the better eye, such as:____

[ ]Abnormal neuroimaging documenting damage to the cerebral cortex, which would be expected to prevent the development of a visual acuity better than 20/200 in the better eye, such as:

____

[ ]Abnormal electroretinogram documenting the presence of:_____________________

[ ] Absent response to Visual Evoked Response (VER) testing in the better eye.

Additional Comments:

____

____

Physician's Name: ____________________Physician's Signature: ____________________

SSA-102.03-VISUAL FIELD CONTRADICTION IN THE BETTER EYE WITH:

Patient Name:____ Date of Exam:______________

Based on the results of the patient's visual field examination, please check all that apply:

[ ] A. The widest diameter subtends an angle around the point of fixation no greater than 20 degrees.

[ ] B. Mean Deviation (MD) of 22 decibels or greater, determined by automated static threshold perimetry that measures the central 30 degrees of the visual field (see 102.00A6d).

[ ] C. A visual field efficiency of 20 percent or less, determined by kinetic perimetry (see 102.00A7c).

Additional Comments::

____

____

____

Physician's Name: ________________________Physician's Signature: ________________________

SSA-102.04-VISUAL EFFICIENCY OR VISUAL IMPAIRMENT IN THE BETTER EYE

Patient Name:____ Date of Exam:______________

Best-Corrected Visual Efficiency Percentage (See 102.00A7d)

- ☐ Visual efficiency percentage is greater than 20%
- ☐ Visual efficiency percentage is 20% or less

Best-Corrected Visual Impairment Value (See 102.00A8d)

- ☐ Visual impairment value is less than 1.00
- ☐ Visual impairment value is 1.00 or greater

Additional Comments:

____

____

____

Supporting Documentation:

☐ Visual acuity test results ☐ Visual field test results ☐ Other relevant medical records (specify): ____

Physician's Name: ________________________Physician's Signature: ________________________

SSA-102.10-LOSS NOT TREATED WITH COCHLER IMPLANTATION

Patient Name:____ Date of Exam:______________

For children from birth to the attainment of age 5:

Does the child have an average air conduction hearing threshold of 50 decibels (dB) or greater in the better ear?

[] Yes [] No

For children from age 5 to the attainment of age 18-Does the child have:

An average air conduction hearing threshold of 70 decibels (dB) or greater in the better ear?

[] Yes [] No

AND an average bone conduction hearing threshold of 40 decibels (dB) or greater in the better ear?

[] Yes [] No

Does the child have a word recognition score of 40 percent or less in the better ear, determined using a standardized list of phonetically balanced monosyllabic words?

[] Yes [] No

Does the child have an average air conduction hearing threshold of 50 decibels (dB) or greater in the better ear?

[] Yes [] No

AND does the child have a marked limitation in speech or language?

[] Yes [] No

Additional Comments:

____

____

____

Physician's Name: ________________________Physician's Signature: ________________________

SSA-102.11-HEARING LOSS TREATED WITH COCHLEAR IMPLANTATION

Patient Name:____ Date of Exam:______________

Has the patient undergone cochlear implantation?

☐ Yes ☐ No

If yes, provide the date of initial implantation: ____

Is the patient under the age of 5?

☐ Yes ☐ No

Has it been at least one year since the initial cochlear implantation?

☐ Yes ☐ No

If the patient is under age 5 OR it has been less than one year since implantation, the patient is considered under a disability.

Section B: Post-Implantation Word Recognition Assessment

(Complete this section if the patient has reached age 5 or it has been at least one year since implantation.)

Has a word recognition test been conducted?

☐ Yes ☐ No

If yes, indicate the test used:

☐ Hearing in Noise Test (HINT) ☐ Hearing in Noise Test for Children (HINT-C)

Word recognition score (%): ____

If the word recognition score is 60 percent or less, the patient meets the criteria for disability under 102.11.

Physician's Name: ________________________Physician's Signature: ________________________

SSA-103.02-CHRONIC RESPIRATORY DISORDERS

Patient Name:____ Date of Exam:______________

Has the patient undergone spirometry testing?

☐ Yes ☐ No

If yes, provide FEV1 value: ____________ L (BTPS)

Patient's Height Without Shoes: ____________ cm / ____________ inches

Does the FEV1 value meet or fall below the threshold in Table I-A or I-B based on patient's age, gender, and height?

☐ Yes ☐ No

Forced Vital Capacity (FVC):

Has the patient undergone spirometry testing?

☐ Yes ☐ No

If yes, provide FVC value: _________________ L (BTPS)

Does the FVC value meet or fall below the threshold in Table II-A or II-B based on patient's age, gender, and height? ☐ Yes ☐ No

Oxygen Supplementation3. Does the patient require continuous (24-hour) oxygen supplementation of at least 1.0 L per minute for at least 90 consecutive days?

☐ Yes ☐ No

If yes, date supplementation began: ____________________

Does the patient have a tracheostomy?

☐ Yes ☐ No

If yes, date of placement: ____________________

If the patient is age 3 or older, is there documented need for mechanical ventilation via tracheostomy for at least 4 hours per day for at least 90 consecutive days?

☐ Yes ☐ No

Chronic Lung Disease (CLD) for Children Under Age 26. Has the patient (under age 2) been diagnosed with Chronic Lung Disease (CLD)?

☐ Yes ☐ No

If yes, has the patient experienced at least 3 hospitalizations within a 12-month period, each lasting at least 48 hours (including emergency room stays prior to admission), with at least 30 days between hospitalizations? ☐ Yes ☐ No

If yes, list hospitalization dates:

1st:__________ 2nd:__________ 3rd:__________ Date of last hospital discharge:__________

Physician's Name: ____________________ Physician's Signature: ____________________

SSA-103.03-ASTHMA

Patient Name:______________________________ Date of Exam:__________

Does the patient have a diagnosis of asthma?

[ ]-Yes [ ]-No

Date of Diagnosis: ______________________________

Has the patient experienced asthma exacerbations requiring hospitalization?

[ ] Yes [ ] No

Number of hospitalizations for asthma within the past 12 months: __________

List dates of hospitalizations and duration:

Hospitalization 1: Date: ______________ Duration: ______________

Hospitalization 2: Date: ______________ Duration: ______________

Hospitalization 3: Date: ______________ Duration: ______________

(Attach additional pages if necessary)

Did each hospitalization last at least 48 hours, including time in the emergency department?

[ ] Yes [ ] No

Were the hospitalizations at least 30 days apart?

[ ] Yes [ ] No

Were there any complications related to these hospitalizations?

[ ] Yes, if so what were they?______________________________

[ ] No

Date of discharge from the most recent hospitalization: ______________

Is the patient currently experiencing any residual impairments related to asthma?

[] Yes [] No

Does the patient require ongoing medical treatment, including medication, oxygen therapy, or other interventions?

[] Yes, if so what intervention?____

[] No

Has the patient's asthma resulted in any limitations in daily activities, school attendance, or exertional capacity?

[] Yes, if so what limitations?____

[] No

In your medical opinion, does the patient continue to meet the criteria under SSA Listing 103.03?

[] Yes [] No

Should their condition be evaluated under another listing?

[] Yes [] No

Physician's Name: __________________________ Physician's Signature: __________________________

SSA-103.04-CYSTIC FIBROSIS

Patient Name:____ Date of Exam:______________

FEV1 (see 103.00E) less than or equal to the value in Table III-A or Table III-B for age, gender, and height without shoes (see 103.00E3a).

[ ] Yes [ ] No

For children under age 6, findings on imaging (see 103.00D3) of thickening of the proximal bronchial airways, nodular-cystic lesions, segmental or lobular atelectasis, or consolidation, AND documentation of one of the following:

[ ] Shortness of breath with activity

[ ] Accumulation of secretions as manifested by repetitive coughing

[ ] Bilateral rales or rhonchi, or reduction of breath sounds

[ ] None of the above

Exacerbations or complications requiring three hospitalizations of any length within a 12-month period and at least 30 days apart.

[ ] Yes [ ] No

Spontaneous pneumothorax, secondary to CF, requiring chest tube placement.

[ ] Yes [ ] No

Respiratory failure requiring:

[] Invasive mechanical ventilation for a continuous period of at least 48 hours

[] Noninvasive ventilation with BiPAP for a continuous period of at least 48 hours

[] Combination of both treatments for a continuous period of at least 48 hours

[] Ventilation for a continuous period of at least 72 hours postoperatively

[] None of the above

Pulmonary hemorrhage requiring vascular embolization to control bleeding.

[] Yes [] No

Two of the following exacerbations or complications within a 12-month period:(Select all that apply)

[] Pulmonary exacerbation requiring 10 consecutive days of intravenous antibiotic treatment

[] Pulmonary hemorrhage requiring hospitalization of any length

[ ] Weight loss requiring daily supplemental enteral nutrition via a gastrostomy for at least 90 consecutive days

[] Weight loss requiring parenteral nutrition via a central venous catheter for at least 90 consecutive days

[] CFRD requiring daily insulin therapy for at least 90 consecutive days

[] None of the above

Physician's Name: ________________________ Physician's Signature: ________________________

SSA-103.06-GROWTH FAILURE DUE TO CHRONIC RESPIRATORY DISORDER

Patient Name:____ Date of Exam:____________

Diagnosis: ____

Does the patient require at least 1.0 L per minute of oxygen supplementation for at least 4 hours per day and for at least 90 consecutive days?

[] Yes [] No

If Yes, please provide details:____

For children from birth to age 2:

Are there three weight-for-length measurements that meet the following criteria?

-Within a consecutive 12-month period

-At least 60 days apart

-Less than the third percentile on the appropriate weight-for-length table under 105.08B1

[] Yes [] No

If Yes, please provide measurement dates and percentiles:

Date 1: _______________ Percentile: ____________%

Date 2: _______________ Percentile: ____________%

Date 3: _______________ Percentile: ____________%

105.08B1

For children age 2 to 18:Are there three BMI-for-age measurements that meet the following criteria?

Within a consecutive 12-month period

At least 60 days apart

Less than the third percentile on the appropriate BMI-for-age table under 105.08B2

[] Yes [] No

If Yes, please provide measurement dates and percentiles:

Date 1: _______________ BMI Percentile: ________%

Date 2: _______________ BMI Percentile: ________%

Date 3: _______________ BMI Percentile: ________%

Physician's Name: ______________________Physician's Signature: ____________________

SSA-103.11-LUNG TRANSPLANTATION EVALUATION

Patient Name:_________________________ Date of Exam:__________

Has the patient undergone a lung transplant?

[] Yes [] No

Date of lung transplantation: _________________________

Is the patient within 3 years of the lung transplant date?

[] Yes [] No

Does the patient have any residual impairments related to the lung transplant?

[] Yes [] No

Does the patient have any symptoms or complications?

[] Yes [] No

Symptoms/Complications:_________________________

____

Does the patient have limitations?

[] Yes [] No

Limitations:_________________________

Is the patient able to engage in full-time work-related activities?

[] Yes [] No

Additional Comments:_________________________

____

Physician's Name: _______________ Physician's Signature: _______________

SSA-103.14-RESPIRATORY FAILURE EVALUATION

Patient Name:______________________________________ Date of Exam:_____________

Does Your Patient Have An Underlying Chronic Respiratory Disorder?

[] Yes [] No

Does Your Patient's Respiratory Failure Require Mechanical Ventilation?

[] Yes [] No

Did Your Patient Experience Postoperative Respiratory Failure?

[] Yes [] No

What is the Frequency of Respiratory Failure Episodes? ______________________________

Additional Comments:

____

____

____

Physician's Name: ____________________Physician's Signature: ____________________

SSA-104.02-CHRONIC HEART FAILURE

Patient Name:_______________________________________ Date of Exam:______________

Does the patient exhibit symptoms consistent with chronic heart failure as described in SSA Listing 104.00C2 (e.g., fatigue, shortness of breath, limited exercise tolerance, or other relevant signs)?

[] Yes [] No

If yes, please describe the symptoms and provide clinical observations:

____

____

Persistent Tachycardia at Rest

[] Yes [] No

If yes, please provide the heart rate readings and corresponding dates (refer to Table I for age-appropriate thresholds):

Date:_________________________ Heart Rate (bpm):________________________

Persistent Tachypnea at Rest or Markedly Decreased Exercise Tolerance

[] Yes [] No

If checked, provide relevant clinical observations, respiratory rate measurements, or exercise test results (refer to Table II):

Date:______________________Respiratory Rate (breaths per minute):___________________

Observations on Exercise Tolerance____

Does the patient have documented growth failure as defined below?

[] Yes [] No

For Children Under Age 2-Three weight-for-length measurements within a 12-month period, at least 60 days apart, and below the 3rd percentile (refer to Tables I or II under 105.08B1).

1-Date:____________ Weight:_________________________ Length________________________

2-Date:____________ Weight:_________________________ Length________________________

3-Date:____________ Weight:_________________________ Length________________________

For Children Age 2 to 18Three BMI-for-age measurements within a 12-month period, at least 60 days apart, and below the 3rd percentile (refer to Tables III or IV under 105.08B2).

1-Date:____________ Weight:_________________________ Length_____________________

2-Date:____________ Weight:_________________________ Length_____________________

3-Date:____________ Weight:_________________________ Length_____________________

Additional Comments:

____

____

____

Physician's Name: ________________________Physician's Signature: ________________________

SSA-104.05-RECURRENT ARRHYTHMIAS

Patient Name:____ Date of Exam:______________

Primary Diagnosis: Recurrent Arrhythmias-ICD Code (if known): __________________________

Underlying Cause:____

Has the patient experienced recurrent episodes of cardiac syncope or near syncope?

____

____

Frequency of episodes:

____

Are these episodes uncontrolled despite prescribed treatment?

[ ] Yes [ ] No

If no treatment is prescribed, please explain:

____

Describe the patient's symptoms related to arrhythmias (check all that apply):

[ ] palpitations [ ] dizziness [ ] fainting [ ] Other ______________

Have the arrhythmias been documented:

[ ] Yes [ ] No

Was the testing conducted during or coincident with the occurrence of syncope or near syncope?

[ ] Yes [ ] No

Is the patient receiving prescribed treatment for arrhythmias?

[ ] Yes [ ] No

If yes, list medications or therapies:

____

Has the prescribed treatment improved the frequency or severity of symptoms?

[ ] Yes [ ] No

If no or partial improvement, please explain:

____

Does the patient experience limitations in daily activities due to recurrent arrhythmias?

[ ] Yes [ ] No

If yes, describe the limitations:

____

Physician's Name: ______________________ Physician's Signature: ______________________

SSA-104.06-CONGENITAL HEART DISEASE

Patient Name:_______________________________________ Date of Exam:____________

Has the patient been diagnosed with congenital heart disease?

[ ] Yes [ ] No

Diagnosis confirmed by:___________________________Date of Diagnosis: ____________

Does the patient have cyanotic heart disease with persistent, chronic hypoxemia?

[ ] Yes [ ] No

If yes, please indicate the following criteria met:_______________________________

____

Does the patient have secondary pulmonary vascular obstructive disease?

[ ] Yes [ ] No

If yes, provide the following details:

Pulmonary arterial systolic pressure: ______ mmHg

Systemic arterial systolic pressure: ______ mmHg

Percentage of pulmonary pressure relative to systemic pressure: ______%

Does the patient have symptomatic acyanotic heart disease?

[ ] Yes [ ] No

If yes, describe the nature of the ventricular dysfunction and how it interferes with the ability to initiate, sustain, or complete activities:_____________________________________

Is the patient under 12 months of age with a life-threatening congenital heart impairment?

[ ] Yes [[No

If yes, please provide supporting information:

____

Has surgical treatment been required or planned in the first year of life?

[ ] Yes [ ] No

Date of surgery (if applicable): ____

Expected duration of impairment and recovery time: ___________________________

Additional Comments:

____

Physician's Name: _____________________Physician's Signature: ____________________

SSA-104.09-HEART TRANSPLANT EVALUATION

Patient Name:______________________________________ Date of Exam:______________

Date of Heart Transplant Surgery: ____

Hospital/Facility where the surgery was performed: _____________________________________

Current Status Post-Transplant: ____

Has the patient experienced any complications?

[] Yes [] No

If complications occurred, please describe their nature, severity, and any resulting functional limitations:____

Medications prescribed for immunosuppression:

Drug(s): ____

Dosage/Frequency: ____

Side effects impacting daily functioning: ____

Most recent cardiac assessment (e.g., echocardiogram, stress test, etc.):

Date: _______________Test performed: ____

Results (include ejection fraction, if available): ____

Does the patient experience symptoms such as fatigue, shortness of breath, or chest pain during daily activities?

[] Yes [] No

If yes, describe: ____

New York Heart Association (NYHA) Functional Classification (check all that apply):

[ ] Class I No limitation of physical activity/no symptoms of heart failure

[ ] Class II Slight limitation of physical activity/Symptoms of heart failure with moderate exertion

[ ] Class III Marked limitation of physical activity/Symptoms of heart failure with minimum exertion

[ ] Class IV Inabiliy to carry out any physical activity without discomfort/Symptoms of heart failure at rest.

Is the patient limited in their ability to perform age-appropriate activities (e.g., school, play, or other daily activities)?

[ ] Yes [ ] No

If yes, describe the limitations: ______________________________

Are there any other medical conditions or complications impacting the patient's functional capacity?

[ ] Yes [ ] No

If yes, describe: ______________________________

Overall prognosis following the transplant:______________________________

____

In your medical opinion, does the patient have significant limitations that are expected to last 12 months or longer?

[ ] Yes [ ] No

Additional Comments:______________________________

____

Physician's Name: ______________________Physician's Signature: ______________________

SSA-104.13-RHEUMATIC HEART DISEASE

Patient Name:____________________________________ Date of Exam:____________

Clinical Findings-Presence of Rheumatic Fever Activity:

Are there significant murmurs present?

[] Yes [] No

If yes, please describe: ____

Cardiac Enlargement or Ventricular Dysfunction:

Associated Abnormal Laboratory Findings / Elevated Sedimentation Rate (ESR):

[] Yes [] No

If yes, provide value and date: ____

ECG Findings:

[] Normal [] Abnormal

If abnormal, describe findings: ____

Has the rheumatic fever activity persisted for 6 months or more within a 12-month period?

[] Yes [] No

If yes, provide supporting documentation and timeline:_____________________________

Does the patient have any functional limitations related to their heart condition (e.g., reduced exercise tolerance, shortness of breath)?

[] Yes [] No

If yes, describe: ____

Medications and Treatment:

List current medications, dosages, and any side effects:

Medication________________________________ Dose________________________________

Side Effects____

Medication________________________________ Dose________________________________

Side Effects____

Medication________________________________ Dose________________________________

Side Effects____

Medication________________________________ Dose________________________________

Side Effects____

Medication________________________________ Dose________________________________

Side Effects____

Medication________________________________ Dose________________________________

Side Effects____

Describe any past or current treatments for rheumatic fever/heart disease:____________________

____

Based on your clinical evaluation and the medical evidence, does the patient's condition meet the criteria described for Rheumatic Heart Disease?

[ ] Yes [ ] No

Additional Comments:____

____

Physician's Name: ________________________Physician's Signature: ________________________

SSA-105.02-GASTROINTESTINAL HEMMORRHAGING

Patient Name:____ Date of Exam:______________

Primary Diagnosis: ____

Underlying Cause of Gastrointestinal Hemorrhaging (if known):

☐ Peptic Ulcer Disease ☐ Esophageal Varices ☐ Gastric or Intestinal Tumor

☐ Inflammatory Bowel Disease ☐ Other (specify): ______________________________

Has the patient required blood transfusions due to gastrointestinal hemorrhaging?

☐ Yes ☐ No

If Yes, please provide details below:

Date of Transfusion	Volume (cc) per kg	Interval Between Transfusions (Days)
_______________	_______________	_______________
_______________	_______________	_______________
_______________	_______________	_______________

Did the patient receive at least three blood transfusions of at least 10 cc of blood/kg per transfusion within a consecutive 12-month period and at least 30 days apart?

☐ Yes ☐ No

Has the patient experienced ongoing symptoms or complications related to gastrointestinal hemorrhaging? [ ]-Yes [ ]-No

☐ Fatigue ☐ Anemia ☐ Hypotension ☐ Weakness

☐ Other (specify): ____

Date of last documented blood transfusion: ____

Based on your medical assessment, does the patient require further evaluation of residual impairments after one year from the last transfusion?

☐ Yes ☐ No

If Yes, please describe any ongoing impairments:

____

____

Physician's Name: ______________________Physician's Signature: ______________________

SSA-105.05-CHRONIC LIVER DISEASE (CLD)

Patient Name:____ Date of Exam:_______________

Has the patient experienced hemorrhaging from varices or portal hypertensive gastropathy?

[] Yes [] No

If yes, provide imaging documentation: ____

Did the hemorrhage result in hemodynamic instability (check all that apply)?

[]-No

[] Yes, as evidenced by:

[] pallor (pale skin) [] diaphoresis (profuse perspiration) [] rapid pulse

[] low blood pressure [] syncope (fainting)

[] postural hypotension (pronounced fall in blood pressure when arising to an upright position from lying down)

[] other: ____

Did the patient require hospitalization for transfusion of at least 10 cc of blood/kg body weight?

[] Yes [] No

Has the patient had ascites or hydrothorax on two evaluations at least 60 days apart within a 12-month period as documented by:

[]-1. Paracentesis; or

[]-2. Thoracentesis; or

[] 3. Imaging or physical examination with a or b:

[] a. Serum albumin of 3.0 g/dL or less; or

[] b. INR of at least 1.5

Has the patient had spontaneous bacterial peritonitis documented by peritoneal fluid neutrophil count ≥ 250 cells/mm3?

[] Yes [] No

Does the patient have hepatorenal syndrome documented by (check all that apply)?

[] Serum creatinine elevation of at least 2 mg/dL; or

[] Oliguria with 24-hour urine output less than 1 mL/kg/hr; or

[] Sodium retention with urine sodium less than 10 mEq per liter.

Does the patient have hepatopulmonary syndrome documented by?:

[] Arterial P_aO_2 measured by an ABG test, while at rest, breathing room air, less than or equal to:

- [] 60 mm Hg, at test sites less than 3,000 feet above sea level; or
- [] 55 mm Hg, at test sites from 3,000 through 6,000 feet above sea level; or
- [] 50 mm Hg, at test sites over 6,000 feet above sea level; or

[] Intrapulmonary arteriovenous shunting as shown on contrast-enhanced echocardiography or macroaggregated albumin lung perfusion scan.

Has the patient exhibited on two evaluations at least 60 days apart within a 12- month period (check all that apply):

[] abnormal behavior [] cognitive dysfunction [] altered mental status

Supporting documentation (check all that apply):

[] History of transjugular intrahepatic portosystemic shunt (TIPS) or other surgical portosystemic shunt

One of the following on at least two evaluations at least 60 days apart within the same consecutive 12-month period:

[] Asterixis or other fluctuating physical neurological abnormalities

[] EEG demonstrating triphasic slow wave activity

[] Serum albumin of 3.0 g/dL or lessr

[] INR of 1.5 or greater.

Two SSA CLD scores of at least 20 within a 12-month period and at least 60 days apart?

[] Yes [] No

For patients <12 years:

One SSA CLD-P score $\geq$ 11?

[] Yes [] No

Has the patient been diagnosed with extrahepatic biliary atresia based on (check one)?

[] Liver biopsy [] intraoperative cholangiogram

Physician's Name: ______________________ Physician's Signature: ______________________

SSA-105.06-INFLAMMATORY BOWEL DISEASE (IBD)

Patient Name:____ Date of Exam:______________

Has the patient been diagnosed with Inflammatory Bowel Disease (IBD)?

☐ Yes ☐ No

If yes, please indicate the method(s) of diagnosis (check all that apply):

☐ Endoscopy ☐ Biopsy ☐ Imaging ☐ Operative Findings

☐ Other (please specify): ____

Has the patient experienced obstruction of stenotic areas (not adhesions) in the small intestine or colon with proximal dilatation?

☐ Yes ☐ No

If yes, was the obstruction confirmed by:

☐ Imaging ☐ Surgery

Has the patient required at least two hospitalizations for intestinal decompression or surgery within a consecutive 12-month period, with at least 60 days between hospitalizations?

☐ Yes ☐ No

If yes, please provide dates of hospitalizations:

First hospitalization date: ____

Second hospitalization date: ____

Has the patient experienced at least two of the following within a consecutive 12-month period and at least 60 days apart? (Check all that apply and provide dates of evaluations where applicable.)

☐ Anemia with hemoglobin less than 10.0 g/dL on at least two evaluations

Date of first evaluation: ____________________Date of second evaluation:____________________

☐ Serum albumin of 3.0 g/dL or less on at least two evaluations

Date of first evaluation: ____________________Date of second evaluation:____________________

☐ Clinically documented tender abdominal mass palpable on physical examination with abdominal pain or cramping

Date of examination: ____

☐ Perianal disease with a draining abscess or fistula

Date of diagnosis: ____

☐ Need for supplemental daily enteral nutrition via gastrostomy, duodenostomy, or jejunostomy, or daily parenteral nutrition via a central venous catheter

Date of initiation: ____

Type of nutrition support: ____

Additional Comments:____

____

Physician's Name: ________________________Physician's Signature: ________________________

SSA-105.07-INTESTINAL FAILURE

Patient Name:____ Date of Exam:______________

Does the patient have a diagnosis of intestinal failure?

☐ Yes ☐ No

Underlying condition(s) contributing to intestinal failure (check all that apply):

☐ Short bowel syndrome ☐ Chronic motility disorder

☐ Extensive small bowel mucosal disease ☐ Other (please specify): ____________________

Date of diagnosis: ____

Does the patient require daily parenteral nutrition via a central venous catheter?

☐ Yes ☐ No

Date parenteral nutrition was initiated: ____

Has the patient been dependent on daily parenteral nutrition for at least 12 months?

☐ Yes ☐ No

Please describe the patient's symptoms related to intestinal failure:

[ ] malabsorption [ ] chronic diarrhea [ ] dehydration [ ] electrolyte imbalances

[ ] other: ____

Does the patient experience complications from parenteral nutrition (e.g., infections, catheter-related complications, liver dysfunction)?

☐ Yes ☐ No

If yes, please describe:____

Does the patient experience significant limitations in daily activities due to their condition?

☐ Yes ☐ No

If yes, please describe:____

Does the patient require frequent medical monitoring or hospitalizations?

☐ Yes ☐ No

If yes, how often? ____

Is the patient's condition expected to improve with treatment?

☐ Yes ☐ No ☐ Uncertain

Any additional medical information relevant to the patient's condition:

____

____

Physician's Name: __________________________Physician's Signature: __________________________

SSA-105.08-GROWTH FAILURE DUE TO DIGESTIVE DISORDER

Patient Name:_________________________ Date of Exam:__________

Has the patient demonstrated chronic nutritional deficiency as documented in at least two evaluations within a consecutive 12-month period and at least 60 days apart?

[ ] Yes [ ] No

If yes, please indicate which criteria apply (check all that apply):

[ ] Anemia with hemoglobin less than 10.0 g/dL [ ] Serum albumin of 3.0 g/dL or less

[ ] Other: ______________________________

Has the patient demonstrated growth failure as required in one of the following categories?
For children from birth to age 2
Three weight-for-length measurements that meet all the following:
Measurements taken within a consecutive 12-month period
Measurements at least 60 days apart
Measurements less than the third percentile values in Table I or Table II

Date__________ Weight__________________ Length______________

Date__________ Weight__________________ Length______________

Date__________ Weight__________________ Length______________

Additional
Comments:______________________________

For children age 2 to attainment of age 18.
Three BMI-for-age measurements that are:
Within a consecutive 12-month period; and
At least 60 days apart; and
Less than the third percentile value in Table III or Table IV.

Date__________ Weight__________________ Length______________

Date__________ Weight__________________ Length______________

Date__________ Weight__________________ Length______________

Additional
Comments:______________________________

Physician's Name: ________________ Physician's Signature: ______________

SSA-105.09-LIVER TRANSPLANT

Patient Name:____________________________________ Date of Exam:______________

Has the patient undergone a liver transplantation?

[ ] No [ ] Yes

Date of liver transplantation: ____

Medical facility where transplantation was performed: ________________________________

Primary diagnosis leading to transplantation: ______________________________________

Were there any complications during or after the transplantation?

[ ] No [ ] Yes (please describe): ____

____

Has the patient experienced any post-transplant complications?

[ ] No [ ] Yes (please describe):____

____

Current immunosuppressive therapy: (List medications and dosages):

Medication____________________________ Dosage____________________________

Medication____________________________ Dosage____________________________

Medication____________________________ Dosage____________________________

Medication____________________________ Dosage____________________________

Medication____________________________ Dosage____________________________

Medication____________________________ Dosage____________________________

Current liver function test results (if available):

AST: __________________ IU/L ALT: __________________ IU/L

Bilirubin (Total/Direct): __________________ mg/dL Albumin: ______________ g/dL

INR: ________________________________

Does the patient demonstrate significant residual impairments related to the transplant?

[] No [] Yes (please describe): ____________________

Does the patient have limitations in daily activities due to the transplantation or residual impairments?

[] No [] Yes (please describe): ____________________

Is the patient able to attend school regularly?

[] Yes [] No

Anticipated prognosis and recovery expectations:____________________

____

____

Physician's Name: ____________________Physician's Signature: ____________________

SSA-105.10-ENTERAL FEEDING VIA GASROSTOMY, DUODENOSTOMY, OR JEJUNOSTOMY

Patient Name:________________________ Date of Exam:__________

What is the primary diagnosis necessitating enteral feeding?

☐ Neurological disorder ☐ Gastrointestinal disorder ☐ Metabolic disorder

☐ Other: ________________________

Date of gastrostomy, duodenostomy, or jejunostomy placement: __________

Has enteral feeding been required daily since placement? ☐ Yes ☐ No

Expected duration of enteral feeding:

☐ Temporary (<12 months) ☐ Indefinite (>12 months)

Is the enteral feeding the sole source of nutrition?

☐ Yes ☐ No

If no, what percentage of daily caloric intake is met through enteral feeding? __________%

Does the child have difficulty tolerating enteral feeds? ☐ No ☐ Yes (describe complications)

[ ] vomiting [ ] aspiration [ ] Infections

[ ] Other ________________________

Does the child exhibit failure to thrive despite enteral feeding?

☐ No ☐ Yes (please describe)________________________

Are there associated growth or developmental delays?

☐ No ☐ Yes (please describe)________________________

Are there comorbid conditions affecting feeding ability (e.g., oral-motor dysfunction, dysphagia)?

☐ No ☐ Yes (please describe)________________________

Is continued enteral feeding necessary beyond age 3?

☐ No ☐ Yes

If yes, what are the expected residual impairments? (Check all that apply)

☐ Growth failure ☐ Swallowing dysfunction ☐ Recurrent aspiration ☐ Severe GERD

☐ Other: ________________________

Physician's Name: ______________Physician's Signature: ______________

SSA-105.11-SMALL INTESTINE TRANSPLANTATION

Patient Name:______________________________ Date of Exam:____________

Date of Small Intestine Transplant: ______________________________

Hospital/Facility Where Transplant Was Performed: ______________________

Indication for Transplant: ______________________________

Has the patient experienced any of the following complications? (Check all that apply)

☐ Organ rejection ☐ Chronic infections ☐ Graft-versus-host disease

☐ Intestinal failure requiring TPN ☐ Other (please specify): ____________

Is the patient currently on immunosuppressive therapy?

☐ Yes ☐ No

Does the patient have any residual impairments related to the transplant?

☐ No ☐ Yes-If yes, describe: ______________________________

____

Are there any limitations on physical activity?

☐ No ☐ Yes-If yes, please explain: ______________________________

____

Does the patient require ongoing medical supervision?

☐ No ☐ Yes

If yes, describe the type and frequency of necessary care: ____________

____

As of one year post-transplant, does the patient have ongoing complications that impact daily activities or ability to work?

☐ No ☐ Yes-If yes, explain: ______________________________

Expected duration of impairment: ______________________________

Physician's Name: ________________Physician's Signature: ________________

SSA-105.12-PANCREAS TRANSPLANTATION

Patient Name:_____________________________________ Date of Exam:_____________

Primary diagnosis necessitating pancreas transplantation:

☐ Type 1 Diabetes Mellitus ☐ Type 2 Diabetes Mellitus ☐ Chronic Pancreatitis

☐ Other: ____

Date of pancreas transplantation: ____

Were there any complications during or after the transplant?

☐ No ☐ Yes (describe): ____

Is the patient currently under medical care for transplant management?

☐ Yes ☐ No

Is the patient on immunosuppressive therapy?

☐ No ☐ Yes (list medications): ____

Has the patient experienced any of the following complications post-transplant? (Check all that apply)

☐ Organ rejection ☐ Infection ☐ Kidney dysfunction ☐ Cardiovascular issues

☐ Other: ____

Does the patient have any residual impairments related to the transplant?

☐ No ☐ Yes (describe): ____

Does the patient have any restrictions on physical activity due to the transplant or related complications?

☐ No ☐ Yes (describe): ____

Is the patient able to engage in full-time work activities?

☐ Yes ☐ No (explain): ______________________________

Based on your medical opinion, does the patient continue to have significant impairments 12 months post-transplant?

☐ No ☐ Yes (explain): ______________________________

Additional comments or recommendations:

____

Physician's Name: ____________________ Physician's Signature: ____________________

SSA-106.03-CHRONIC KIDNEY DISEASE (CKD) WITH CHRONIC HEMODIALYSIS OR PERITONEAL DIALYSIS

Patient Name:____ Date of Exam:______________

Does the patient have a diagnosis of Chronic Kidney Disease (CKD)?

☐ No ☐ Yes-If yes, date of diagnosis: ____

Is the patient currently undergoing chronic hemodialysis or peritoneal dialysis?

☐ Yes, hemodialysis ☐ Yes, peritoneal dialysis ☐ No

If yes, when did dialysis treatment begin? Date: _________________

How frequently does the patient receive dialysis treatments?

☐ 3 times per week ☐ Other (please specify): _________________________________

Where does the patient receive dialysis?

☐ Outpatient dialysis center ☐ Home dialysis

☐ Other (please specify): ____

Has the patient been prescribed dialysis on a chronic and ongoing basis?

☐ Yes ☐ No

Has the patient experienced complications related to CKD or dialysis (e.g., peritonitis, infections, cardiovascular issues)?

☐ No ☐ Yes (please describe): ____

Does the patient have laboratory findings confirming end-stage renal disease (ESRD)?

☐ Yes ☐ No

Does the patient have other conditions or impairments related to CKD (e.g., hypertension, neuropathy, bone disease)?

☐ No ☐ Yes (please specify): ____

Does the patient experience significant fatigue or weakness related to CKD or dialysis?

☐ Yes ☐ No

Does the patient have activity limitations due to CKD or dialysis (e.g., ability to attend school, engage in daily activities)?

☐ No ☐ Yes (please describe): ______________________________

Has the patient been hospitalized due to CKD complications in the past 12 months?

☐ No ☐ Yes, number of hospitalizations: ______________________________

Is the patient expected to require ongoing dialysis indefinitely?

☐ Yes ☐ No

Additional comments regarding the patient's condition and limitations:

____

____

Physician's Name: ______________________Physician's Signature: ______________________

SSA-106.04-CHRONIC KIDNEY DISEASE (CKD) WITH KIDNEY TRANSPLANT

Patient Name:______________________________________ Date of Exam:____________

Date of Kidney Transplant: ____

Current status of kidney function: ____

Has the patient experienced any episodes of rejection?

[] No [] Yes (please describe)____

Have there been any complications in other body systems related to the transplant?

[] No [] Yes (please describe)____

Is the patient on immunosuppressive therapy?

[] No [] Yes (please describe)____

Current estimated glomerular filtration rate (eGFR): _____________________________

Serum Creatinine: ____

Blood Urea Nitrogen (BUN): ____

Has the patient experienced?:

[ ] recurrent infections (describe)____

[ ] cardiovascular issues (describe)____

[ ] post-transplant complications?(describe)________________________________

Does the patient require dialysis post-transplant?

[ ] Yes [ ] No

Has the patient's ability to perform daily activities been affected post-transplant?

[ ] No [ ] Yes (describe)____

Was the patient's CKD severe enough to meet the definition of disability prior to transplant?

[ ] No [ ] Yes (describe)____

Considering the patient's post-transplant condition, do you anticipate that they will continue to experience significant limitations after the one-year post-transplant period?

[[No [ ] Yes

Physician's Name: ______________________ Physician's Signature: ____________________

SSA-106.05-CHRONIC KIDNEY DISEASE (CKD) WITH IMPAIRMENT OF KIDNEY FUNCTION

Patient Name:______________________________________ Date of Exam:____________

Does the patient have a diagnosis of chronic kidney disease (CKD)?

[] No [] Yes (what stage of CKD?)________________________________

Has the patient had at least two of the following laboratory findings, documented at least 90 days apart within a consecutive 12-month period?:

[] No [] Yes

Serum Creatinine Level of 3mg/dl or greater

[] Yes [] No

Creatinine Clearance of 30 ml/min/1.73m2 or less

[] Yes [] No

Estimated Glomerular Filtration Rate (eGFR) of 30 ml/min/1.73m2 or less

[] Yes [] No

Has the patient undergone dialysis treatment?

[] Yes [] No

Does the patient have other complications related to CKD such as:

[] hypertension [] anemia [] bone disease

[] Other (describe)____

Physician's Name: ______________________Physician's Signature: ______________________

SSA-106.06-NEPHROTIC SYNDROME

Patient Name:____ Date of Exam:______________

Laboratory Findings(Documentation required on at least two occasions at least 90 days apart within a consecutive 12-month period)

Serum Albumin Levels:

1st Measurement (Date: _______________) _______________ g/dL

2nd Measurement (Date: ______________) _________________ g/dL(Must be 3.0 g/dL or less)

Proteinuria Levels:

1st Measurement (Date: ____________) _______________ mg/m²/hr

2nd Measurement (Date: ____________) _______________ mg/m²/hr(Must be 40 mg/m²/hr or greater)

Anasarca (Generalized Massive Edema)(Persisting for at least 90 days despite prescribed treatment)

Extent of Edema:

Pretibial Edema (in front of tibia):

[] Yes [] No

Periorbital Edema (around eyes):

[]Yes [] No

Presacral Edema (in front of sacrum):

[] Yes [] No

Additional Conditions (Check all that apply and provide details):

[ ] ascites (describe)____

[ ] pleural effusion (describe)____

[ ] pericardial effusion (describe)____

Prescribed treatment:

____

____

Duration of treatment:

____

____

Patient response to treatment:

[ ] Improved [ ] No Improvement [ ] Worsened

Additional comments:

____

____

Physician's Name: ________________________Physician's Signature: ________________________

SSA-106.07-CONGENITAL GENITOURINARY DISORDER

Patient Name:______________________________________ Date of Exam:______________

Does the patient have a congenital genitourinary disorder?

☐ No ☐ Yes If yes, please specify the diagnosis: ______________________________

Please describe the nature and severity of the disorder:______________________________

____

Has the patient undergone urologic surgical procedures at least three times within a consecutive 12-month period, with at least 30 days between procedures?

☐ No ☐ Yes If yes, please provide details:

Date of Surgery	Type of Procedure	Hospital/Facility

Were any of the procedures diagnostic cystoscopy or circumcision?

☐ Yes ☐ No

What is the expected recovery time following the most recent surgery?______________________

Are there any residual impairments following the last surgery?

☐ No ☐ Yes (describe)____

Is the patient expected to require additional urologic surgeries in the future?

☐ No ☐ Yes (specify anticipated procedures/timeframe:______________________

____

Physician's Name: ______________________Physician's Signature: ______________________

SSA-106.08-GROWTH FAILURE DUE TO CHRONIC RENAL DISEASE

Patient Name:____ Date of Exam:______________

Has the patient been diagnosed with chronic renal disease?
[ ] No [ ] Yes-If yes, specify diagnosis: ________________________________

Has the patient had serum creatinine levels of 2 mg/dL or greater on at least two occasions within a consecutive 12-month period, with at least 60 days between measurements?
[ ] No [ ] Yes-If yes, provide the following details:

Date of 1st Measurement:	Serum Creatinine Level: mg/dL
Date of 2nd Measurement:	Serum Creatinine Level mg/dL

Date of 1st measurement: _________________Serum creatinine level:_________________ mg/dL

Date of 2nd measurement: _________________Serum creatinine level: ________________ mg/dL

For children from birth to age 2:
Has the child had three weight-for-length measurements within a consecutive 12-month period, at least 60 days apart, and less than the third percentile on the appropriate weight-for-length table?
[ ] No [ ] Yes-If yes, provide the following details:

Date of 1st Measurement:	Weight for Length Percentile:
Date of 2nd Measurement:	Weight for Length Percentile:
Date of 3rd Measurement:	Weight for Length Percentile:

For children age 2 to 18:
Has the child had three BMI-for-age measurements within a consecutive 12-month period, at least 60 days apart, and less than the third percentile on the appropriate BMI-for-age table?
[ ] No [ ] Yes-If yes, provide the following details:

Date of 1st Measurement:	BMI-for-age percentile:
Date of 2nd Measurement:	BMI-for age percentile:
Date of 3rd Measurement	BMI-for age percentile:

Physician's Name: ________________________Physician's Signature: ________________________

SSA-106.09-COMPLICATIONS OF CHRONIC KIDNEY DISEASE (CKD)

Patient Name:____ Date of Exam:_______________

Has the individual been diagnosed with chronic kidney disease?

[] Yes [] No

Have there been at least three hospitalizations related to complications of chronic kidney disease within a consecutive 12-month period?

[] Yes [] No

Did each hospitalization occur at least 30 days apart?

[] Yes [] No

Did each hospitalization last at least 48 hours, including time spent in the emergency department before admission?

[] Yes [] No

Please provide the dates and durations of each hospitalization:

Hospitalization 1: Date: ______________________ Duration: ________________________

Hospitalization 2: Date: ______________________ Duration: ________________________

Hospitalization 3: Date: ______________________ Duration: ________________________

Has the individual been diagnosed with growth failure due to chronic renal disease?

[] Yes [] No

Have laboratory findings required under 106.08A been documented within the same 12-month period as growth measurements?

[] Yes [] No

Please provide the dates of laboratory findings:

Date of Lab Test 1:	Serum Creatinine (2mg/dL or +):
Date of Lab Test 2:	Serum Creatinine (2mg/dL or +)

Growth Measurements

Please provide the child's growth measurements within the same 12-month period:

Height:	Date:
Weight:	Date:

Is the child's growth measurement below the third percentile based on the appropriate table under 105.08B?

[] Yes [] No

BMI Evaluation (for children age 2 to 18)

Has the child's BMI been evaluated according to the BMI-for-age table?

[] Yes [] No

Please provide the BMI calculation:

Weight (kg or lbs):	Height (cm or in):	BMI Calculation:

Does the child's BMI fall below the third percentile for their age and gender?

[] Yes [] No

Physician's Name: ________________________ Physician's Signature: ________________________

SSA-107.05-HEMOLYTIC ANEMIAS (INCLUDING SICKLE CELL DISEASE AND THALASSEMIA)

Patient Name:_______________________________________ Date of Exam:_____________

Diagnosis:

☐ Sickle Cell Disease ☐ Thalassemia

☐ Other Hemolytic Anemia Variant (specify): _______________________________________

Has the patient experienced documented painful (vaso-occlusive) crises requiring parenteral (IV or IM) narcotic medication?

☐ No ☐ Yes-If yes, how many times in the past 12 months? ______________________

Were the crises at least 30 days apart?

☐ Yes ☐ No

Has the patient been hospitalized due to complications of hemolytic anemia?

☐ No ☐ Yes-If yes, how many hospitalizations in the past 12 months? _____________

Were the hospitalizations at least 30 days apart?

☐ Yes ☐ No

Did each hospitalization last at least 48 hours, including emergency department time?

☐ No ☐ Yes

Reasons for hospitalization:

[ ] dactylitis [ ] osteomyelitis [ ] acute chest syndrome [ ] Other:_____________

Has the patient had hemoglobin measurements of 7.0 g/dL or less?

☐ No ☐ Yes-If yes, provide dates and levels:

Date:	Level g/dL
Date:	Level g/dL
Date:	Level g/dL

Were these measurements taken at least 30 days apart?

☐ Yes ☐ No

Does the patient require life-long RBC transfusions to maintain life?

☐ Yes ☐ No

Frequency of RBC transfusions:

☐ Every 6 weeks ☐ Other (specify): ______________________________

Does the patient experience functional limitations due to their condition?

☐ No ☐ Yes -If yes, describe limitations and associated symptoms: ______________

____

Are there any complications related to transfusions

[] No

[] Yes (check all that apply below)

[] iron overload [] infections) [] Other: ______________________

Additional Comments:______________________________________

____

Physician's Name: ______________________ Physician's Signature: ______________________

SSA-107.08-DISORDERS OF THROMBOSIS & HEMOSTASIS

Patient Name:____ Date of Exam:______________

Does the patient have a diagnosed disorder of thrombosis and hemostasis (e.g., hemophilia, thrombocytopenia)?
[ ] No [ ] Yes-If yes, please specify the diagnosis: ________________________________
Date of initial diagnosis: ____
Please describe the nature and severity of the patient's disorder:
____

Has the patient required at least three hospitalizations within a 12-month period, occurring at least 30 days apart?
[ ] No [ ] Yes-If yes, please complete the following:

Date of Hospitalization	Length of Stay(Hours)	Reason for admission

Did any of these hospitalizations include emergency department care or treatment in a comprehensive hemophilia treatment center immediately prior to admission?
[ ] No [ ] Yes-If yes, please describe: ____

Please describe the complications that led to hospitalization:_______________________________
____

Has the patient undergone any surgeries within the past 12 months?
[ ] No [ ] Yes-If yes, please provide details:

Type of Surgery	Date of Surgery

Was clotting-factor protein (e.g., Factor VIII or IX) or anticoagulant medication required to manage bleeding or coagulation?
[ ] No [[Yes

Please provide any additional relevant information regarding the patient's disorder, treatment needs, or prognosis:____
____

Physician's Name: ________________________ Physician's Signature: ______________________

SSA-107.10-DISORDERS OF BONE MARROW FAILURE

Patient Name:_______________________________________ Date of Exam:_____________

Does the patient have a diagnosed disorder of bone marrow failure?
[] No [] Yes-Date of initial diagnosis: ______________________________

Diagnostic tests confirming the disorder:
[] bone marrow biopsy [] blood tests [] other: ____________________

Has the patient experienced complications of bone marrow failure requiring at least three hospitalizations within a 12-month period, occurring at least 30 days apart?
[] No [] Yes-If yes, please provide details of each hospitalization:

Hospitalization Date	Duration (at least 48 hours)	Complication requiring Hospitalization

Were any of the hospitalizations preceded by emergency department treatment?
[] No [] Yes-If yes, please provide details: ______________________________

Does the patient have a diagnosis of myelodysplastic syndrome or aplastic anemia requiring life-long RBC transfusions at least once every six weeks to maintain life?
[] No [] Yes-If yes, please provide details:______________________________

Date RBC transfusion therapy began: ______________________________
Frequency of transfusions: ______________________________
Medical necessity for continued transfusions: ______________________________

Are the RBC transfusions required for life maintenance similar to the requirement in beta thalassemia major?
[] Yes [] No-If no, please explain: ______________________________

Please provide any additional information relevant to the patient's condition, including response to treatment, prognosis, or other factors affecting functionality:

____

Physician's Name: ______________________Physician's Signature: ______________________

SSA-107.17-HEMETOLOGICAL DISORDERS TREATED BY BONE MARROW OR STEM CELL TRANSPLANTATION

Patient Name:______________________________________ Date of Exam:____________

Type of transplant performed: Date of Diagnosis:___________

[ ] Bone Marrow Transplant [ ] Stem Cell Transplant

Underlying hematological disorder requiring transplantation: ____________________________

Pre-transplant treatments received:

[ ] chemotherapy [ ] radiation [ ] immunotherapy [ ] Other __________________

Has the patient experienced any serious complications post-transplantation?

[ ] No [ ] YesIf yes, please check all applicable complications:

[ ] Graft-versus-host (GVH) disease [ ] Frequent infections after immunosuppressive therapy

[ ] Significant deterioration of organ systems [ ] Other serious complications (please describe):

____

____

Does the patient continue to experience significant impairments affecting daily activities, mobility, or organ function?

[ ] No [ ] Yes-If yes, describe the functional limitations and affected body systems:

____

____

Based on medical evidence, do you believe the patient remains disabled beyond the initial 12-month period post-transplantation?

[ ] No [ ] Yes If yes, please explain the medical reasons supporting continued disability status:

____

____

Physician's Name: ____________________Physician's Signature: ____________________

SSA-108.07-PHOTOSENSITIVITY DISORDERS

Patient Name:____ Date of Exam:______________

Does the patient have a confirmed diagnosis of a genetic photosensitivity disorder?

☐ No ☐ Yes, specify the diagnosis:

☐ Xeroderma Pigmentosum (XP)

☐ Other Genetic Photosensitivity Disorder (please specify): ________________________________

____

Does the patient have chronic skin lesions?

☐ No ☐ Yes, If yes, describe the severity, frequency, and affected areas:

____

____

Does the patient have contractures?

☐ No ☐ Yes, If yes, specify the affected joints and functional limitations:

____

____

Does the patient require a highly protective environment to prevent worsening of their condition? ☐

☐ No ☐ Yes, If yes, describe the protective measures required: ______________________

____

☐ The patient cannot use both upper extremities to independently initiate, sustain, and complete age-appropriate fine and gross motor activities due to chronic skin lesions or contractures.

☐ The patient cannot use one upper extremity for fine and gross motor activities and requires an assistive device with the other upper extremity.

☐ The patient cannot stand up from a seated position and maintain an upright posture due to chronic skin lesions or contractures affecting at least two extremities (including perineum/inguinal region).

☐ The patient cannot maintain an upright position while standing or walking due to chronic skin lesions or contractures affecting both lower extremities (including perineum/inguinal region).

☐ The patient experiences chronic pain or other limitations resulting in significant functional impairment. If yes, describe the pain severity, frequency, and its impact on daily functioning:

____

____

Does the patient require continuous medical treatment or therapy for their condition?

☐ No ☐ Yes, If yes, describe the type and frequency of treatment: ________________

____

Are there any additional functional impairments not covered above?

☐ No ☐ Yes, If yes, describe: ______________________________________

____

Physician's Name: ______________________Physician's Signature: ______________________

SSA-108.08-BURNS

Patient Name:____ Date of Exam:________________

Does the patient have a history of burns that required surgical management?

[] No [] Yes

If yes, has the patient reached maximum therapeutic benefit and no longer requires surgical management?

[] No [] Yes

Are there chronic skin lesions or contractures resulting from the burns?

[] No [] Yes

Functional Limitations Please check all that apply:
[] Involve use of your wrists, hands, and fingers
[] Include picking, pinching, manipulating, and fingering
[] Involve use of your shoulders, upper arms, forearms, and hands
[] Include handling, gripping, grasping, holding, turning, and reaching
[] Include exertional activities such as lifting, carrying, pushing, and pulling

Does the patient experience chronic pain associated with the burns that significantly impacts functional ability?

[] No [] Yes

If yes, please describe the severity, frequency, and treatment of the pain:

Severity: ____

Frequency: ____

Treatment of the Pain: ____

Does the patient require ongoing medical treatment, therapy, or assistive devices?

[] No [] Yes-If yes, please specify:

Medical Treatment: ____

Therapy: ____

Assistive Devices: ____

Physician's Name: _________________________Physician's Signature: __________________________

SSA-108.09-CHRONIC CONDITIONS OF THE SKIN OR MUCOUS MEMBRANES

Patient Name:____________________________________ Date of Exam:____________

Has your Patient been diagnosed with a Chronic Skin or Mucous Membrane Condition?

☐ No ☐ Yes-If yes, specify the diagnosis: ______________________________

____

Does the patient have chronic skin lesions or contractures?

☐ No ☐ Yes-If yes, describe the nature, location, and severity of the lesions or contractures:

____

____

____

Has the patient adhered to prescribed medical treatment for at least 3 months?

☐ No ☐ Yes-If yes, describe treatment provided and response:____________________

____

____

Does the patient continue to experience chronic pain or other physical limitations despite treatment?

☐ No ☐ Yes-If yes, describe the limitations:____________________________

____

____

Does the patient have impairment-related functional limitations?

☐ No ☐ Yes-If yes, check all that apply:

☐ Inability to use both upper extremities to independently initiate, sustain, and complete age-appropriate activities involving fine and gross movements.

☐ Inability to use one upper extremity to independently initiate, sustain, and complete age-appropriate activities, and a documented medical need for an assistive device that requires use of the other upper extremity.

☐ Inability to stand up from a seated position and maintain an upright position to the extent needed to independently initiate, sustain, and complete age-appropriate activities due to chronic skin lesions or contractures affecting at least two extremities.

☐ Inability to maintain an upright position while standing or walking to the extent needed to independently initiate, sustain, and complete age-appropriate activities due to chronic skin lesions or contractures affecting both lower extremities.

Please provide additional details regarding the functional limitations checked above:_____________

____

____

In your professional opinion, how do the patient's chronic skin or mucous membrane conditions impact their ability to perform daily activities?____

____

____

Are there any additional medical conditions or factors that exacerbate the patient's limitations?

☐ No ☐ Yes-If yes, explain:____

____

____

Do you believe the patient meets the criteria for 108.09 based on your medical evaluation?

☐ No ☐ Unsure ☐ Yes-If yes, please provide a medical rationale for this determination: ____

____

____

Physician's Name: __________________________Physician's Signature: __________________________

SSA-109.08-DIABETES MELLITUS IN CHILDREN

Patient Name:_______________________________________ Date of Exam:_______________

Type of Diabetes Mellitus (DM) Diagnosed:____________________Date of Diagnosis: ____________

Does the child require daily insulin therapy?

[ ] No [ ] Yes

Does the child require 24-hour-a-day adult supervision for insulin management, food intake, and physical activity to ensure survival?

[ ] No [ ] Yes-If Yes, please describe: ____

____

Does the child experience frequent episodes of hyperglycemia?

[ ] No [ ] Yes-If Yes, approximate frequency:____________________________________

Has the child experienced long-term complications of hyperglycemia?

[ ] No [ ] Yes-If Yes, please specify: ____

____

Has the child had any episodes of Diabetic Ketoacidosis (DKA) requiring hospitalization?

[ ] No [ ] Yes-If Yes, how many episodes in the past 12 months? ____________________

Were any complications associated with DKA?

[ ] No [ ] Yes-If Yes, specify:

[ ] cardiac arrhythmias [ ] cerebral edema [ ] seizures [ ] other ________________

____

Does the child experience frequent episodes of hypoglycemia?

[] No [] Yes-If yes, approximate frequency:______________________________

____

Has the child experienced severe hypoglycemic episodes?

[] No [] Yes-If yes, have the severe hypoglycemic episodes led to:

[] seizures [] Loss of consciousness [] Cognitive deficits or permanent brain damage

[] Other: ____

Does the child have difficulty managing their diabetes?

[] No [] Yes-If yes was it due to:

[] Hypoglycemia unawareness

[] Other medical disorders affecting glucose levels

[] Mental disorders impacting diabetes management

[] Inadequate treatment compliance due to cognitive or psychosocial factors

[] Other:____

Does the child require additional accommodations or assistance at school or home?

[] No [] Yes-If Yes, describe: ______________________________________

____

Additional Comments:____

____

Physician's Name: ________________________Physician's Signature: ____________________

SSA-110.06-NON-MOSAIC DOWN SYNDROME (CHROMOSOME 21 TRISOMY OR CHROMOSOME 21 TRANSLOCATION)

Patient Name:______________________________________ Date of Exam:______________

Does the patient have a laboratory-confirmed diagnosis of non-mosaic Down syndrome (chromosome 21 trisomy or chromosome 21 translocation)?

[ ] No [ ] Yes

Please provide documentation of karyotype analysis:______________________________________

____

Does the patient have a physician-confirmed diagnosis of chromosome 21 trisomy or chromosome 21 translocation based on prior karyotype analysis and clinical features?

[ ] No [ ] Yes

Does the patient have distinctive facial or other physical features consistent with Down syndrome?

[ ] No [ ] Yes

If prior karyotype analysis is unavailable, does the patient's functioning align with a diagnosis of non-mosaic Down syndrome based on medical and nonmedical evidence such as:

[ ] physical and mental abilities [ ] developmental history [ ] educational background

[ ] psychological testing [ ] other: ______________________________________

If available, please provide supporting evidence of the patient's condition:____________________

____

In your professional opinion, does the patient meet the criteria for non-mosaic Down syndrome?

[ ] No [ ] Yes

Physician's Name: ______________________Physician's Signature: ____________________

SSA-110.08-CATASTROPHIC CONGENITAL DISORDERS

Patient Name:____ Date of Exam:______________

Does the patient have a diagnosed catastrophic congenital disorder?

[ ] No [ ] Yes-If yes, specify the disorder: ______________________________________

____

Is the disorder expected to result in early death (within the first months of life)?

[ ] No [ ] Yes

Does the disorder cause very serious interference with development or functioning?

[ ] No [ ] Yes-If yes describe: ____

____

List the characteristic physical and clinical features observed:_______________________

____

____

Describe any significant developmental or functional impairments related to the disorder:________

____

____

Physician's Name: ______________________Physician's Signature: ______________________

SSA-111.02-EPILEPSY

Patient Name:____ Date of Exam:______________

Diagnosis: ____ Date of Diagnosis:__________

Does the patient's typical seizure episode include?:

[ ] aura-describe____

[ ] duration-describe____

[ ] postictal state____

[ ] recovery time ____

Type(s) of seizures observed/documented (check all that apply):

☐ Generalized tonic-clonic seizures ☐ Dyscognitive seizures ☐ Absence seizures

☐ Other (please specify): ____

____

Frequency of Seizures (despite adherence to prescribed treatment):

☐ Generalized tonic-clonic seizures occurring at least once a month for at least 3 consecutive months

☐ Dyscognitive or absence seizures occurring at least once a week for at least 3 consecutive months

☐ Other frequency (please specify): ________________________________

____

Is the patient prescribed antiseizure medication?

☐ No ☐ Yes-If yes, list current medications and dosages:

____

____

In your medical opinion, is the patient adherent to prescribed treatment?

☐ Yes ☐ No

Despite adherence to prescribed treatment, do the patient's seizures continue to meet the frequency criteria listed above?

☐ Yes ☐ No

Are there any other medical conditions that impact the patient's seizure disorder?

☐ No ☐ Yes (please describe): ______________________________

____

Any additional comments:

____

____

Physician's Name: ________________________ Physician's Signature: ________________________

SSA-111.04-VASCULAR INSULT TO THE BRAIN

Patient Name:______________________________________ Date of Exam:______________

Does the patient have a history of a vascular insult to the brain?

[ ] No [ ] Yes-If yes

[ ] stroke- date of insult__________________[ ] cerebral hemorrhage-date of insult________________

Does the patient exhibit disorganization of motor function in two extremities?

[ ] No [ ] Yes-If yes, affected extremities:____

Does the patient experience extreme limitation in any of the following? (Check all that apply):

[ ] inability to stand up from a seated position

[ ] maintain balance in a standing position and while walking

[ ] using upper extremities to independently initiate, sustain and complete age appropriate activities.

Has the above limitation(s) persisted for at least 3 consecutive months after the vascular insult?

[ ] No [ ] Yes

The severity of motor dysfunction and its impact on the patient's daily activities includes:

[ ] need for assistive device

[ ] caregiver assistance

[ ] inability to perform fine motor tasks

[ ] inability to perform gross motor tasks

Does the patient require any assistive devices for mobility?

[ ] No [ ] Yes-what is the assistive device?: ______________________________________

Does the patient require?:

[ ] ongoing therapy [ ] rehabilitation services?

Additional comments:

____

____

Physician's Name: _________________________Physician's Signature: _______________________

SSA-111.05-BENIGN BRAIN TUMORS

Patient Name:______________________________________ Date of Exam:____________

Does the patient have a benign brain tumor? Date of Diagnosis:__________

☐ No ☐ Yes; If yes, provide the diagnosis: ______________________________

Diagnostic methods used:

☐ MRI ☐ CT Scan ☐ Neurological Examination

☐ Other: ____

Does the patient have disorganization of motor function in two extremities, resulting in an extreme limitation?

☐ No ☐ Yes; If yes, indicate which extremities are affected:

☐ Both lower extremities ☐ Both upper extremities

☐ One upper extremity and one lower extremity

Does the patient have an extreme limitation in the ability to stand up from a seated position?

☐ No ☐ Yes; If yes, does the patient require assistance from:

[ ] another person to stand [ ] an assistive device (e.g., walker, two crutches, two canes) to stand

Describe clinical findings supporting this limitation: ______________________________

____

Does the patient have an extreme limitation in the ability to balance while standing or walking?

☐ No ☐ Yes; If yes, does the patient require assistance from:

[ ] another person [[an assistive device

Describe clinical findings supporting this limitation: ______________________________

____

Does the patient have an extreme limitation in the ability to use the upper extremities?

☐ No ☐ Yes; If yes, which of the following abilities are severely limited? (Check all that apply):

☐ Pinching, manipulating, and using fingers

☐ Handling, gripping, grasping, holding, turning, reaching

☐ Lifting, carrying, pushing, pulling

Describe clinical findings supporting this limitation: ____________________________________

____

Does the patient's impairment interfere with the ability to independently initiate, sustain, and complete age-appropriate activities?

☐ No ☐ Yes; If yes, please explain: ____

____

What treatment(s) has the patient received for this condition?

☐ Medication (list): ____

☐ Physical therapy

☐ Surgery (date and type): ____

☐ Other (specify): ____

Has the patient's condition improved, remained stable, or worsened over time?

☐ Improved ☐ Stable ☐ Worsened; If worsened, describe progression: ______________

____

Please provide any additional medical findings, observations, or relevant information:___________

____

____

Physician's Name: _______________________Physician's Signature: ______________________

SSA-111.07-CEREBRAL PALSY

Patient Name:_______________________________________ Date of Exam:_____________

Diagnosis: ____Date of Diagnosis:__________

Does the patient have disorganization of motor function in two extremities due to cerebral palsy:

[ ] both lower extremities

[ ] both upper extremities

[ ] one upper and one lower extremity

Does the patient have an extreme limitation in any of the following abilities? (Check all that apply):

[ ] inability to stand up from a seated position

[ ] assistance from a person or assistive device to stand up

[ ] assistance from a person or assistive device to maintain an upright position from a seated position

Does the patient require assistance to maintain balance while standing or walking?

[ ] from another person [ ] from an assistive device; type of device:___________________

Does the patient have loss of function in both upper extremities that very seriously limits their ability to independently initiate, sustain, and complete age-appropriate activities involving fine and gross motor movements?

[ ] No [ ] Yes-If yes, which specific motor functions are impaired? (Check all that apply):

[ ] unable to pinch, manipulate, and use your fingers

[ ] unable to use your hands, arms, and shoulders to perform gross motor movements

[ ] unable to handle, grip, grasp, hold, turn, and reach

[ ] unable to lift, carry, push, and pull

Physician's Name: _____________________Physician's Signature: ______________________

SSA-111.08-SPINAL CORD DISORDERS

Patient Name:____ Date of Exam:______________

Does the patient have a diagnosed spinal cord disorder?
[ ] No [ ] Yes; if yes, provide diagnosis: ____

Date of onset of symptoms: ________________Date of confirmed diagnosis: ________________

Does the patient have a complete loss of function for three consecutive months?
[ ] No [ ] Yes; If yes:
[ ] motor function-affected area ____
[ ] sensory function-affected area ______________________________________
[ ] autonomic function-affected area ____________________________________

Does the patient have disorganization of motor function in two extremities?
[ ] No [ ] Yes; if yes, indicate the affected extremities:_____________________________________
____

Does the patient have an extreme limitation in the ability to?:
[ ] Stand up from a seated position
[ ] Balance while standing or walking
[ ] Use the upper extremities

If limitations exist, do they persist for at least 3 consecutive months after the disorder?
[ ] No
[ ] Yes-if yes:
[ ] inability to stand up from a seated position
[ ] inability to maintain balance while standing or walking
[ ] inability to use upper extremities:

Are there objective medical findings supporting the diagnosis and functional limitations?
[ ] No [ ] Yes; if yes, indicate types of evidence available:__________________________________
____

Has there been any improvement in the patient's condition?
[ ] No [ ] Yes

Physician's Name: ________________________Physician's Signature: ________________________

SSA-111.09-COMMUNICATION IMPAIRMENT

Patient Name:____________________________________ Date of Exam:____________

Does the patient have a medically determinable neurological disorder?

[] No

[] Yes; If yes, Diagnosis: ____________________________Date of Diagnosis _________

Diagnostic Tests Performed: ____

Treating Specialist(s): ____

Does the patient have a documented speech deficit that significantly affects the clarity and content of their speech?

[] No [] Yes; If yes, please describe the nature of the speech deficit:__________________

____

How does the speech deficit impact the patient's ability to communicate?________________

____

Does the patient have a documented comprehension deficit resulting in ineffective verbal communication for their age?

[] No [] Yes; If yes, please describe the comprehension deficit:______________________

____

How does the comprehension deficit affect the patient's ability to communicate?____________

____

Does the patient have an impairment of hearing?

[] No [] Yes

Degree of hearing loss: ____

Audiometric findings: ____

Use of hearing aids or cochlear implants: _________________________________

Has the patient undergone a comprehensive communication evaluation?

[ ] No [ ] Yes-If yes, please provide the date and evaluator's name:

Date:_______________ Evaluator: _____________________________________

Summary of findings:____

____

Based on your assessment, how does the patient's communication impairment impact daily functioning?____

____

Are there any recommended treatments, therapies, or accommodations?__________________

____

Physician's Name: ______________________Physician's Signature: _________________

SSA-111.12-MYASTHENIA GRAVIS

Patient Name:______________________________________ Date of Exam:_____________

Has the patient been diagnosed with Myasthenia Gravis?
[] No [] Yes; If yes, date of diagnosis: ______________________________

Has the patient been adherent to prescribed treatment for at least three consecutive months?
[] Yes [] No; if no, please explain: ______________________________
____

Has the patient's condition continued to meet the criteria below despite adherence to treatment?
[] No [] Yes

Does the patient exhibit disorganization of motor function in two extremities, resulting in extreme limitation?
[] No [] Yes

If present, describe the extent and impact of motor function disorganization:
[] limited ability to stand up from a seated position
[] limited ability to balance while standing or walking
[] limited ability to use the upper extremities
____
____

Does the patient exhibit bulbar and neuromuscular dysfunction?
[] No [] Yes
[] bulbar dysfunction [] neuromuscular dysfunction
If present, describe the severity and frequency of these impairments:____________________
____

Does the patient have an extreme limitation in the ability to:
[] breathe [] swallow [] speak [] Other: ____________________
If applicable, please describe the specific limitations observed:____________________
____

Additional Comments: ____
____

Physician's Name: ______________________Physician's Signature: ____________________

SSA-111.13-MUSCULAR DYSTROPHY

Patient Name:____ Date of Exam:______________

Does the patient have a diagnosis of muscular dystrophy? Date of diagnosis: ______________

☐ No ☐ Yes; If yes, please specify type: ____

Confirmatory tests performed (check all that apply):

☐ Genetic testing ☐ Muscle biopsy ☐ Electromyography (EMG)

☐ Creatine kinase (CK) levels ☐ Other: ____

Does the patient have disorganization of motor function in at least two extremities (both lower extremities, both upper extremities, or one upper extremity and one lower extremity)?

☐ No

☐ Yes; If yes, please specify which extremities are affected:

☐ Both lower extremities ☐ Both upper extremities

☐ One upper extremity and one lower extremity

Does the patient have extreme limitation in any of the following abilities?

[ ] Standing Up from a Seated Position

Does the patient require assistance to stand up from:

[ ] another person

[ ] assistive device

[ ] walker

[ ] two crutches

[ ] two canes

z[ ] Balance While Standing or Walking

Does the patient require assistance to maintain balance from:

[ ] another person

[ ] assistive device

[ ] walker

[ ] two crutches

[ ] two canes

[ ] Use of Upper Extremities

Does the patient have significant limitations in performing fine and gross motor movements such as:

[ ] Pinching, manipulating, or using fingers

[ ] Handling, gripping, grasping, holding, turning, or reaching

[ ] Lifting, carrying, pushing, or pulling

Does the patient require any of the following assistive devices? (Check all that apply)

☐ Walker ☐ Two crutches ☐ Two canes ☐ Wheelchair

☐ Other: ____________________

Additional Commments: ____________________

____

Physician's Name: ____________________ Physician's Signature: ____________________

SSA-111.14-PERIPHERAL NEUROPATHY

Patient Name:____ Date of Exam:_______________

Does the patient have a diagnosis of peripheral neuropathy?

☐ No ☐ Yes; If yes, please specify the date of diagnosis ______________________________________

Underlying cause (if known): ____

Supporting diagnostic tests

[ ] EMG [ ] NCS [ ] MRI [ ] Clinical exams: ______________________________

Does the patient have disorganization of motor function in two extremities, resulting in an extreme limitation in the ability to:

[ ] Stand up from a seated position [ ] Maintain balance while standing or walking

[ ] Use the upper extremities (e.g., fingers, wrists, hands, arms, shoulders) to initiate, sustain, and complete activities

Does the patient require assistance from another person or an assistive device (e.g., walker, two crutches, two canes) to stand?

☐ Yes ☐ No

Can the patient maintain an upright position while standing or walking without assistance from another person or an assistive device?

☐ Yes ☐ No

Does the patient have significant loss of function in both upper extremities that limits their ability to perform fine and gross motor movements?

☐ No ☐ Yes

If yes, which activities are affected? (Check all that apply)

☐ Pinching, manipulating, or using fingers

☐ Handling, gripping, grasping, holding, turning, reaching

☐ Lifting, carrying, pushing, pulling

☐ Other (please specify): ____

Does the patient require any of the following devices for mobility or stability? (Check all that apply)

☐ Walker ☐ Two crutches ☐ Two canes ☐ Wheelchair

☐ Other (please specify): ____

Physician's Name: ________________________Physician's Signature: ______________________

SSA-111.17-NEURODEGENERATIVE DISORDERS OF THE CENTRAL NERVOUS SYSTEM SUCH AS A JUVENILE-ONSET HUNTINGTON'S DISEASE AND FRIEDREICH'S ATAXIA

Patient Name:____ Date of Exam:_____________

Please indicate the patient's diagnosed neurodegenerative disorder:

☐ Juvenile-onset Huntington's disease ☐ Friedreich's ataxia

☐ Other (please specify): ____

Does the patient have disorganization of motor function in two extremities?

☐ No ☐ Yes, If yes, which extremities are affected?

☐ Both lower extremities

☐ Both upper extremities

☐ One upper and one lower extremity

Does the patient have an extreme limitation in the ability to:

[ ] Stand up from a seated position

[ ] Balance while standing or walking

[ ] Use the upper extremities (e.g., fingers, wrists, hands, arms, shoulders) to independently initiate, sustain, and complete age-appropriate activities

Is the patient unable to stand and maintain an upright position without the assistance of another person or an assistive device (e.g., walker, two crutches, two canes)?

☐ Yes ☐ No

Is the patient unable to maintain an upright position while standing or walking without assistance?

☐ Yes ☐ No

Does the patient experience loss of function in both upper extremities that significantly limits fine and gross motor movements?

☐ No ☐ Yes; if yes, which of the following are affected? (Check all that apply)

☐ Pinching, manipulating, and using fingers

☐ Handling, gripping, grasping, holding, turning, and reaching

☐ Lifting, carrying, pushing, and pulling

Additional Comments: ____

____

Physician's Name: ______________________Physician's Signature: ______________________

SSA-111.18-TRAUMATIC BRAIN INJURY (TBI)

Patient Name:____ Date of Exam:______________

Does the patient have a diagnosed traumatic brain injury (TBI)?

☐ No ☐ Yes; If yes, provide the date of diagnosis: ______________________________

Has the patient experienced disorganization of motor function affecting two extremities due to TBI?

☐ No ☐ Yes; If yes, specify the affected extremities:

☐ Both lower extremities ☐ Both upper extremities

☐ One upper extremity and one lower extremity

How long has the disorganization of motor function persisted?

☐ Less than 3 months ☐ 3 months or longer

Does the patient have an extreme limitation in the ability to stand up from a seated position?

☐ No ☐ Yes; if yes, does the patient require assistance from:

☐ Another person ☐ Assistive device

[ ] walker [ ] two crutches [ ] two canes

Does the patient have an extreme limitation in maintaining balance while standing or walking?

☐ No ☐ Yes; if yes, does the patient require assistance from:

☐ Another person ☐ Assistive device

[ ] walker [ ] two crutches [ ] two canes

Does the patient have an extreme limitation in the use of both upper extremities?

☐ No ☐ Yes, If yes, indicate which functions are impaired (check all that apply):

☐ Pinching, manipulating, and using fingers

☐ Handling, gripping, grasping, holding, turning, and reaching

☐ Lifting, carrying, pushing, and pulling

Are the patient's limitations expected to last for at least 12 months?

☐ Yes ☐ No

Are there any additional factors affecting the patient's motor function (e.g., spasticity, ataxia, weakness)?

☐ No ☐ Yes; If yes, please explain:

[ ] spasticity [ ] ataxia [ ] weakness

Physician's Name: ________________________Physician's Signature: ________________________

SSA-111.20-COMA OR PERSISTENT VEGETATIVE STATE

Patient Name:______________________________________ Date of Exam:______________

Diagnosis Date of Onset:______________

☐ Coma ☐ Persistent Vegetative State ☐ Other (please specify): ____________________

Has the patient remained in a coma or persistent vegetative state for at least one month?

☐ Yes ☐ No

Does the patient demonstrate no evidence of awareness of self or environment?

☐ Yes ☐ No

Does the patient show no purposeful response to stimuli?

☐ Yes ☐ No

Does the patient exhibit no ability to communicate (verbal or non-verbal)?

☐ Yes ☐ No

Are brainstem reflexes present?

☐ Yes ☐ No

Have any imaging studies been performed (e.g., CT scan, MRI, EEG)?

☐ Yes ☐ No

In your medical opinion, is there any likelihood of meaningful neurological recovery?

☐ No ☐ Yes-If yes, describe the expected level of improvement: ____________________

____

Additional Comments:____

____

Physician's Name: ________________________Physician's Signature: ________________________

SSA-111.21-MULTIPLE SCLEROSIS

Patient Name:____ Date of Exam:_______________

Does the patient have a confirmed diagnosis of Multiple Sclerosis?

☐ No ☐ Yes; If yes, date of diagnosis: ____

Diagnostic tests used to confirm MS (check all that apply):

☐ MRI of Brain/Spinal Cord ☐ Lumbar Puncture ☐ Evoked Potentials

☐ Other (please specify): ____

Does the patient exhibit disorganization of motor function in two extremities due to MS, interfering with movement?

☐ No ☐ Yes; If yes, which extremities are affected? (check one)

☐ Both lower extremities

☐ Both upper extremities

☐ One upper and one lower extremity

Please describe the specific impairments observed: ____

____

Does the patient have extreme limitation in their ability to:

Stand up from a seated position?

☐ No ☐ Yes; If yes, describe the limitations: ____

____

Does the patient require assistance from another person or an assistive device (e.g., walker, two crutches, two canes) to stand?

☐ No ☐ Yes

Maintain balance while standing or walking?

☐ No ☐ Yes, if yes, describe the limitations: ______________________________

____

Does the patient require an assistive device to balance?

☐ No ☐ Yes

Use the upper extremities for fine and gross motor functions?

☐ No ☐ Yes; If yes, describe the limitations: ______________________________

____

Examples of affected functions (check all that apply):

☐ Pinching, manipulating, and using fingers

☐ Handling, gripping, grasping, holding, turning, reaching

☐ Lifting, carrying, pushing, pulling

Based on your medical evaluation, describe how the patient's MS impacts their ability to perform daily activities, work-related tasks, or age-appropriate activities:______________________

____

____

Does the patient require any additional medical equipment or accommodations?

☐ No ☐ Yes (please specify):______________________________________

____

Additional Comments:

____

____

Physician's Name: ______________________Physician's Signature: ____________________

SSA-111.22-MOTOR NEURON DISORDERS

Patient Name:_________________________ Date of Exam:__________

Does the patient have a medically documented diagnosis of a motor neuron disorder?

[] No [] Yes-If yes, please specify: ____________________

Does the patient have disorganization of motor function in two extremities (both lower extremities, both upper extremities, or one upper and one lower extremity)?

[] No [] Yes; if yes, which extremities are affected? ____________________

____

Does this disorganization result in an extreme limitation in the ability to:

Stand up from a seated position?

[] No [] Yes

Maintain balance while standing or walking?

[] No [] Yes

Use the upper extremities for fine and gross motor movements?

[] No [] Yes

Describe the degree of interference with the patient's ability to perform these functions:__________

____

____

Does the patient have bulbar and neuromuscular dysfunction?

[] No [] Yes; If yes, does this dysfunction result in any of the following

[] Acute respiratory failure requiring invasive mechanical ventilation

[] Need for supplemental enteral nutrition via a gastrostomy or parenteral nutrition via a central venous catheter

Does the patient have any of the following impairments related to bulbar dysfunction?

[ ] Difficulty breathing [ ] Difficulty swallowing [ ] Difficulty speaking

Does the patient require assistance to stand up from a seated position?

[ ] No [ ] Yes

Does the patient require assistance to maintain balance while standing or walking?

[ ] No [ ] Yes

Does the patient have a loss of function in both upper extremities that severely limits the ability to independently initiate, sustain, and complete age-appropriate activities?

[ ] No [ ] Yes; If yes, which of the following fine and gross motor movements are impaired?

[ ] Pinching, manipulating, and using fingers

[ ] Handling, gripping, grasping, holding, turning, and reaching

[ ] Lifting, carrying, pushing, and pulling

Based on your medical evaluation, describe the overall impact of the patient's motor neuron disorder on their daily activities and functional abilities:________________________________

____

____

Physician's Name: ________________________ Physician's Signature: ________________________

SSA-112.02-NEUROCOGNITIVE DISORDERS

Patient Name:____ Date of Exam:______________

Does the patient have a clinically significant deviation in normal cognitive development or a significant cognitive decline from a prior level of functioning in one or more of the following areas? (Check all that apply):

[] Complex attention [] Executive functioning [] Learning and memory

[] Language [] Perceptual motor [] Social cognition

Does the patient exhibit an extreme limitation of one, or marked limitation of two, of the following areas of mental functioning? (Check all that apply and indicate severity):

[ ] Understand, remember, or apply information (e.g., learning new things, following instructions, applying knowledge to tasks)

[] mild [] moderate [] marked [] extreme

[ ] Interact with others (e.g., responding appropriately to social cues, maintaining relationships, handling conflicts)

[] mild [] moderate [] marked [] extreme

Concentrate, persist, or maintain pace (e.g., focusing on tasks, working at a consistent pace, avoiding distractions):

[] mild [] moderate [] marked [] extreme

Adapt or manage oneself (e.g., regulating emotions, responding to changes, practicing personal hygiene):

[] mild [] moderate [] marked [] extreme

Has the patient's mental disorder been documented for at least 2 years?

[ ] No [ ] Yes

Is there evidence of ongoing treatment, therapy, psychosocial supports, or highly structured settings that help diminish symptoms?

[ ] No [ ] Yes

Does the patient demonstrate marginal adjustment, meaning they have minimal capacity to adapt to changes or new demands?

[ ] No [ ] Yes

Additional Comments:____

____

Physician's Name: ________________________ Physician's Signature: ________________________

SSA-112.04-DEPRESSIVE, BIPOLAR, AND RELATED DISORDERS

Patient Name:______________________________________ Date of Exam:______________

Diagnosis (Check all that apply:

[ ] Depressive disorder [ ] Bipolar disorder [ ] Related disorder

For Depressive Disorder: Check all that apply (must have five or more symptoms):

[ ] Depressed or irritable mood; [ ] Diminished interest in almost all activities;

[ ] Appetite disturbance with change in weight (or a failure to achieve an expected weight gain);

[ ] Sleep disturbance; [ ] Observable psychomotor agitation or retardation;

[ ] Decreased energy; [ ] Feelings of guilt or worthlessness;

[ ] Difficulty concentrating or thinking; [ ] Thoughts of death or suicide.

For Bipolar Disorder: Check all that apply (must have three or more symptoms):

[ ] Pressured speech; [ ] Flight of ideas; [ ] Inflated self-esteem;

[ ] Decreased need for sleep; [ ] Distractibility;

[ ] Involvement in activities that have a high probability of painful consequences that are not recognized

[ ] Increase in goal-directed activity or psychomotor agitation.

For Disruptive Mood Dysregulation Disorder: Check all that apply (all must be present):

[ ] Persistent, significant irritability or anger;

[ ] Frequent, developmentally inconsistent temper outbursts; and

[ ] Frequent aggressive or destructive behavior.

Does the child exhibit extreme limitation in one, or marked limitation in two, of the following areas of mental functioning? (Check all that apply and indicate severity: Extreme or Marked)

[ ] Understand, remember, or apply information

[ ] mild [ ] moderate [ ] marked [ ] extreme

[ ] Interact with others

[ ] mild [ ] moderate [ ] marked [ ] extreme

[ ] Concentrate, persist, or maintain pace

[ ] mild [ ] moderate [ ] marked [ ] extreme

[ ] Adapt or manage oneself

[ ] mild [ ] moderate [ ] marked [ ] extreme

Has the child's mental disorder persisted for at least two years?

[ ] Yes [ ] No

Is there evidence of ongoing?:

Medical treatment, mental health therapy, psychosocial support(s), or a highly structured setting(s) that is ongoing and that diminishes the symptoms and signs of your mental disorder;

[ ] Yes [ ] No

Marginal adjustment, that is, you have minimal capacity to adapt to changes in your environment or to demands that are not already part of your daily life.

[ ] Yes [ ] No

Does the child demonstrate marginal adjustment (minimal capacity to adapt to changes in environment or new demands)?

[ ] Yes [ ] No

Additional Comments:____

____

Physician's Name: ________________________Physician's Signature: ________________________

SSA-112.05-INTELLECTUAL DISORDER

Patient Name:____________________________________ Date of Exam:______________

Is there evidence of significantly subaverage general intellectual functioning such that the child is unable to participate in standardized testing of intellectual functioning?

☐ No

☐ Yes; If yes, please describe the cognitive impairments preventing standardized testing:________

____

____

Does the child have significant deficits in adaptive functioning currently manifested by dependence on others for personal needs (e.g., toileting, eating, dressing, or bathing) beyond age-appropriate dependence?

☐ No

☐ Yes; If yes, please describe the specific deficits in adaptive functioning:__________________

____

____

Has the child undergone standardized testing of intellectual functioning?

☐ No

☐ Yes; if yes, provide the most recent full-scale IQ score: ____________________________

[ ] Is the full-scale IQ score is 70 or below.

[ ] Is the full-scale IQ score is between 71-75; If so, provide the verbal and performance IQ scores:

Verbal IQ Score: _______________ Performance IQ Score: __________

Does the child exhibit significant deficits in adaptive functioning currently manifested by extreme limitation of one, or marked limitation of two, of the following mental functioning areas? (Check all that apply)

☐ Understanding, remembering, or applying information (e.g., learning new material, following instructions, problem-solving)

[ ] No Limitation [ ] Mild [ ] Moderate [ ] Marked [ ] Extreme

☐ Interacting with others (e.g., responding appropriately to authority figures, engaging with peers, making and maintaining friendships)

[ ] No Limitation [ ] Mild [ ] Moderate [ ] Marked [ ] Extreme

☐ Concentrating, persisting, or maintaining pace (e.g., sustaining attention, carrying out tasks with appropriate speed and accuracy)

[ ] No Limitation [ ] Mild [ ] Moderate [ ] Marked [ ] Extreme

☐ Adapting or managing oneself (e.g., handling changes in routine, exhibiting self-control, handling frustration appropriately)

[ ] No Limitation [ ] Mild [ ] Moderate [ ] Marked [ ] Extreme

If any are checked, please provide examples and clinical observations:________________________

____

____

Additional Comments: ____

____

____

Physician's Name: ________________________Physician's Signature: ______________________

SSA-112.06-ANXIETYAND OBSESSIVE-COMPULSIVE DISORDERS

Patient Name:____ Date of Exam:______________

Please indicate the presence of symptoms by checking all that apply:

[ ] Anxiety Disorder, characterized by one or more of the following:

☐ Restlessness ☐ Easily fatigued ☐ Difficulty concentrating ☐ Irritability

☐ Muscle tension ☐ Sleep disturbance

[ ] Panic Disorder or Agoraphobia, characterized by one or both:

☐ Panic attacks followed by a persistent concern or worry about additional panic attacks or their consequences

☐ Disproportionate fear or anxiety about at least two different situations

[ ] using public transportation [ ] being in a crowd [ ] being in a line

[ ] being outside the home [ ] being in open spaces

[ ] other:____

[ ] Obsessive-Compulsive Disorder, characterized by one or both:

☐ Involuntary, time-consuming preoccupation with intrusive, unwanted thoughts

☐ Repetitive behaviors that appear aimed at reducing anxiety

[ ] Separation Anxiety Disorder:

☐ Excessive fear or anxiety concerning separation from those to whom the patient is attached

Please indicate the severity of impairment:

Understand, remember, or apply information

☐No Limitation ☐Mild ☐Moderate ☐Marked ☐Extreme

Interact with others

☐No Limitation ☐Mild ☐Moderate ☐Marked ☐Extreme

Concentrate, persist, or maintain page

☐No Limitation ☐Mild ☐Moderate ☐Marked ☐Extreme

Adapt or manage onself

☐No Limitation ☐Mild ☐Moderate ☐Marked ☐Extreme

Has the patient's condition persisted for at least 12 months?

☐ Yes ☐ No

Is the condition expected to last at least 12 months?

☐ Yes ☐ No

Treatment, Prognosis and Current medications (if any): ____________________

____

Frequency of treatment: ____________________

____

Response to treatment: ____________________

____

Prognosis: ____________________

____

Physician's Name: ____________________ Physician's Signature: ____________________

SSA-112.07-SOMATIC SYMPTOM AND RELATED DISORDERS

Patient Name:____ Date of Exam:______________

Does the patient exhibit one or both of the following (check all that apply)?

[ ] Symptoms of altered voluntary motor or sensory function that are not better explained by another medical or mental disorder

[ ] One or more somatic symptoms that are distressing, with excessive thoughts, feelings, or behaviors related to the symptoms

Please describe the nature, frequency, and severity of the symptoms:

Nature:____

Frequency: ____

Severity: ____

Have these symptoms been evaluated for other medical or mental health conditions that could explain them?

[ ] No

[ ] Yes; What diagnostic tests, if any, have been performed to assess these symptoms?____________

____

What treatments have been attempted, and how has the patient responded?____________________

____

Section B: Mental Functioning Limitations. Please evaluate the severity of the patient's limitations in the following areas of mental functioning, using the following scale:

Understanding, remembering, or applying information (e.g., learning, recalling instructions, problem-solving)

☐No Limitation ☐Mild ☐Moderate ☐Marked ☐Extreme

Please provide an example: ____

____

Interacting with others (e.g., forming relationships, responding to authority, engaging in social interactions)

☐No Limitation ☐Mild ☐Moderate ☐Marked ☐Extreme

Please provide an example:____

____

Concentrating, persisting, or maintaining pace (e.g., focusing, completing tasks, handling routine changes)

☐No Limitation ☐Mild ☐Moderate ☐Marked ☐Extreme

Please provide an example:____

____

Adapting or managing oneself (e.g., handling stress, regulating emotions, maintaining personal hygiene)

☐No Limitation ☐Mild ☐Moderate ☐Marked ☐Extreme

Please provide an example:____

____

Do you believe the patient's condition significantly limits their ability to function in an age-appropriate manner?

[ ] No [ ] Yes; If yes, please describe in detail:______________________________

____

Are there any other medical or psychological conditions that contribute to the patient's limitations?

[ ] No [ ] Yes

Additional Comments: ____

____

____

Physician's Name: ______________________ Physician's Signature: ______________________

SSA-112.08-PERSONALITY AND IMPULSE-CONTROL DISORDERS (Ages 3 to 18)

Patient Name:______________________________________ Date of Exam:______________

Please indicate whether the child exhibits a pervasive pattern of one or more of the following traits. Check all that apply:

☐ Distrust and suspiciousness of others ☐ Detachment from social relationships

☐ Disregard for and violation of the rights of others ☐ Instability of interpersonal relationships

☐ Excessive emotionality and attention seeking ☐ Feelings of inadequacy

☐ Excessive need to be taken care of ☐ Preoccupation with perfectionism and orderliness

☐ Recurrent, impulsive, aggressive behavioral outbursts

For each of the following areas of mental functioning, please indicate the level of limitation:

Understanding, remembering, or applying information:

[ ] No Limitation [ ] Mild [ ] Moderate [ ] Marked [ ] Extreme

Interacting with others:

[ ] No Limitation [ ] Mild [ ] Moderate [ ] Marked [ ] Extreme

Concentrating, persisting, or maintaining pace:

[ ] No Limitation [ ] Mild [ ] Moderate [ ] Marked [ ] Extreme

Adapting or managing oneself:

[ ] No Limitation [ ] Mild [ ] Moderate [ ] Marked [ ] Extreme

Additional Comments:____

____

Physician's Name: ________________________ Physician's Signature: ________________________

SSA-112.10-AUTISM SPECTRUM DISORDER-(Listing 112.10)

Patient Name:______________________________ Date of Exam:____________

Qualitative deficits in communication and social interaction:

Does the child exhibit qualitative deficits in verbal communication?

[] No [] Yes; if yes, please describe: ______________________________

____

____

Does the child exhibit qualitative deficits in nonverbal communication?

[] No [] Yes; if yes, please describe: ______________________________

____

____

Does the child exhibit qualitative deficits in social interaction?

[] No [] Yes; If yes, please describe: ______________________________

____

____

Restricted, repetitive patterns of behavior, interests, or activities:

Does the child engage in repetitive motor movements, use of objects, or speech?

[] No [] Yes; If yes, please describe: ______________________________

____

____

Does the child insist on sameness, exhibit inflexible adherence to routines, or show ritualized patterns of behavior?

[] No [] Yes; If yes, please describe: ______________________________

____

____

Does the child have highly restricted, fixated interests that are abnormal in intensity or focus?

[ ] No [ ] Yes; If yes, please describe: ______________________________

____

____

Does the child display hyper- or hypo-reactivity to sensory input or unusual interest in sensory aspects of the environment?

[ ] No [ ] Yes; If yes, please describe: ______________________________

____

____

Understanding, remembering, or applying information:

[ ] No Limitation [ ] Mild [ ] Moderate [ ] Marked [ ] Extreme

Interacting with others:

[ ] No Limitation [ ] Mild [ ] Moderate [ ] Marked [ ] Extreme

Concentrating, persisting, or maintaining pace:

[ ] No Limitation [ ] Mild [ ] Moderate [ ] Marked [ ] Extreme

Adapting or managing oneself:

[ ] No Limitation [ ] Mild [ ] Moderate [ ] Marked [ ] Extreme

Additional Comments:______________________________

____

____

____

Physician's Name: ______________________________ Physician's Signature: ______________________________

SSA-112.12-NEURODEVELOPMENTAL DISORDERS FOR CHILDREN AGE 3 TO ATTAINMENT OF AGE 18

Patient Name:____ Date of Exam:______________

Does the patient have medical documentation of one or more of the following? (Check all that apply)
[ ] Frequent distractibility, difficulty sustaining attention, and difficulty organizing tasks
[ ] Hyperactive and impulsive behavior such difficulty remaining seated, talking excessively, difficulty waiting, appearing restless, or behaving as if being "driven by a motor"
[ ] Significant difficulties learning and using academic skills
[[Recurrent motor movement or vocalization

Does the patient have an extreme limitation in one, or marked limitation in two, of the following areas of mental functioning? (Check all that apply and indicate severity)

Understanding, remembering, or applying information (e.g., learning new concepts, following instructions, problem-solving):

☐ No limitation ☐ Mild ☐ Moderate ☐ Marked ☐ Extreme

Interacting with others (e.g., engaging in appropriate social interactions, responding to authority figures, maintaining friendships):

☐ No limitation ☐ Mild ☐ Moderate ☐ Marked ☐ Extreme

Concentrating, persisting, or maintaining pace (e.g., staying on task, working independently, maintaining focus for extended periods):

☐ No limitation ☐ Mild ☐ Moderate ☐ Marked ☐ Extreme

Adapting or managing oneself (e.g., regulating emotions, handling changes in routine, self-care, personal safety awareness):

☐ No limitation ☐ Mild ☐ Moderate ☐ Marked ☐ Extreme

Describe any medical or psychological treatments the patient is currently receiving for the above condition(s): ____

____

In your professional opinion, how do these impairments impact the patient's ability to function in an academic or social setting?____

____

Physician's Name: __________________________Physician's Signature: __________________________

SSA-112.13-EATING DISORDERS

Patient Name:____ Date of Exam:_______________

Primary eating disorder diagnosis: ___________________________Date of diagnosis: ____________

Does the patient exhibit a persistent alteration in eating or eating-related behavior?

☐ No ☐ Yes; If yes, please describe the nature of the alteration:_______________________

____

Does the alteration result in a change in food consumption or nutrient absorption?

☐ No ☐ Yes; if yes, please describe how the patient's food intake or absorption is affected:

____

Has the eating disorder significantly impaired the patient's physical health?

☐ No ☐ Yes; If yes, please describe the physical health consequences (e.g., weight loss, malnutrition, electrolyte imbalances, organ dysfunction, hospitalizations, etc.):____________________

____

Has the eating disorder significantly impaired the patient's psychological health?

☐ No ☐ Yes; If yes, please describe the psychological effects (e.g., anxiety, depression, obsessive behaviors, social withdrawal, suicidal ideation, etc.): ______________________________

____

Understanding, Remembering, or Applying Information:
Does the patient have difficulty learning, recalling, or using information?

☐ No Limitation ☐ Mild ☐ Moderate ☐ Marked ☐ Extreme

Interacting with Others:
Does the patient struggle with social interactions, communication, or forming relationships?

☐ No Limitation ☐ Mild ☐ Moderate ☐ Marked ☐ Extreme

Concentrating, Persisting, or Maintaining Pace:
Does the patient experience difficulties in focus, task completion, or sustaining mental effort?

☐ No Limitation ☐ Mild ☐ Moderate ☐ Marked ☐ Extreme

Adapting or Managing Oneself:
Does the patient have difficulty managing emotions, controlling behaviors, or maintaining personal care?

☐ No Limitation ☐ Mild ☐ Moderate ☐ Marked ☐ Extreme

Physician's Name: __________________________Physician's Signature: _________________________

SSA-112.14-DEVELOPMENTAL DISORDERS IN INFANTS AND TODDLERS

Patient Name:_________________________________ Date of Exam:____________

What is the patient's diagnosed developmental disorder_________________________

Is there medical documentation of one or both of the following?

☐ A delay or deficit in the development of age-appropriate skills

☐ A loss of previously acquired skills ☐ Neither

Please describe the specific developmental delays, deficits, or skill losses observed:____________

____

Does the patient exhibit an extreme limitation in at least one, or a marked limitation in at least two, of the following developmental abilities? *(Check all that apply and indicate severity)*

Motor Planning & Control (e.g., difficulty coordinating movements, delays in gross or fine motor skills)

☐ No Limitation ☐ Mild ☐ Moderate ☐ Marked ☐ Extreme

Learning and Memory (e.g., inability to retain new information, severe cognitive delays)

☐ No Limitation ☐ Mild ☐ Moderate ☐ Marked ☐ Extreme

Social Interaction (e.g., difficulty engaging with caregivers, poor eye contact, lack of interest in peers)

☐ No Limitation ☐ Mild ☐ Moderate ☐ Marked ☐ Extreme

Regulation of Physiological Functions, Attention, Emotion, and Behavior (e.g., difficulty self-soothing, excessive irritability, inability to focus)

☐ No Limitation ☐ Mild ☐ Moderate ☐ Marked ☐ Extreme

Are there any other medical, neurological, or environmental factors contributing to the patient's developmental disorder?

☐ No ☐Yes-Explain: ______________________________________

Has the patient undergone any developmental or neuropsychological evaluations?

☐ No ☐ Yes (Date(s) & Findings: ______________________________

Are there any recommended interventions or treatments for the patient's condition?

☐ Speech therapy ☐ Occupational therapy ☐ Physical therapy

☐ Behavioral therapy ☐ Other: ______________________________

Physician's Name: ____________________Physician's Signature: ________________

SSA-112.15-TRAUMA-AND STRESSOR-RELATED DISORDERS

Patient Name:____________________________________ Date of Exam:______________

Diagnosis____

For Post-Traumatic Stress Disorder (PTSD), does the child exhibit all of the following:

[ ] Exposure to actual or threatened death, serious injury, or violence;

[ ]Subsequent involuntary re-experiencing of the traumatic event (for example, intrusive memories, dreams, or flashbacks);

[ ] Avoidance of external reminders of the event;

[ ] Disturbance in mood and behavior (for example, developmental regression, socially withdrawn behavior);

[ ] Increases in arousal and reactivity (for example, exaggerated startle response, sleep disturbance).

For Reactive Attachment Disorder (RAD), does the child exhibit at least two of the following?

[ ] Rarely seeks comfort when distressed; [ ] Rarely responds to comfort when distressed

[ ] Episodes of unexplained emotional distress.

Understanding, remembering, or applying information (e.g., learning new concepts, following instructions, problem-solving):

☐ No Limitation ☐ Mild ☐ Moderate ☐ Marked ☐ Extreme

Interacting with others (e.g., engaging in appropriate social interactions, responding to authority figures, maintaining friendships):

☐ No Limitation ☐ Mild ☐ Moderate ☐ Marked ☐ Extreme

Concentrating, persisting, or maintaining pace (e.g., staying on task, working independently, maintaining focus for extended periods):

☐ No Limitation ☐ Mild ☐ Moderate ☐ Marked ☐ Extreme

Adapting or managing oneself (e.g., regulating emotions, handling changes in routine, self-care, personal safety awareness):

☐ No Limitation ☐ Mild ☐ Moderate ☐ Marked ☐ Extreme

Does the child have a medically documented history of the disorder for at least 2 years?

[ ] No [ ] Yes; If Yes, is there evidence of BOTH of the following?

[ ] Ongoing medical treatment, mental health therapy, psychosocial support, or a highly structured setting that diminishes symptoms:

[ ] Marginal adjustment (minimal capacity to adapt to changes in environment or new demands):

Physician's Name: ______________________ Physician's Signature: ______________________

SSA-113.03-MALIGNANT SOLID TUMORS

Patient Name:____________________ Date of Exam:__________

Has the patient been diagnosed with a malignant solid tumor?

☐ No ☐ Yes; If yes, provide the initial date of diagnosis: __________

Has the malignancy recurred with active disease?

☐ No ☐ Yes; If yes, provide the date of recurrence: __________

Current treatment plan (check all that apply):

☐ Chemotherapy ☐ Radiation ☐ Surgery ☐ Immunotherapy

☐ Other (please specify): __________

Has the patient completed treatment?

☐ Yes, date completed: __________

☐ No, ongoing treatment

Does the patient have any residual impairments following treatment?

☐ No ☐ Yes; If yes, describe the impairments and their impact on functional abilities:

____

____

Affected body system(s):

☐ Neurological ☐ Cardiovascular ☐ Pulmonary ☐ Musculoskeletal

☐ Other: __________

Based on your medical opinion, does the patient meet the criteria for disability?

☐ Yes ☐ No If no, explain your reasoning:

____

____

Physician's Name: __________ Physician's Signature: __________

SSA-113.05-LYMPHOMA (EXCLUDING ALL TYPES OF LYMPHOBLASTIC LYMPHOMA)

Patient Name:____ Date of Exam:_____________

Type of lymphoma diagnosed: Date of Diagnosis_____________

[ ] Non-Hodgkin lymphoma (including Burkitt's and anaplastic large cell)

[ ] Hodgkin lymphoma [ ] Mantle cell lymphoma [ ] Other: _______________

Did the patient have involvement of any of the following at initial diagnosis? (Check all that apply)

[ ] bone marrow [ ] brain [ ] spinal cord [ ] liver [ ] lung

Has the lymphoma been persistent or recurrent following initial anticancer therapy?

[ ] No [ ] Yes; If yes, provide details:____

____

Has the patient undergone bone marrow or stem cell transplantation?

[ ] No [ ] Yes; If yes, are there any residual impairments following transplantation?_______

____

Does the patient have any other impairments related to lymphoma or its treatment?

[ ] No [ ] Yes; If yes, describe:____

____

Physician's Name: ______________________Physician's Signature: ______________________

SSA-113.06-LEUKEMIA

Patient Name:____ Date of Exam:______________

Diagnosis and Classification Date of Diagnosis:______________

☐ Acute leukemia (including all types of lymphoblastic lymphoma and juvenile chronic myelogenous leukemia (JCML))

☐ Chronic myelogenous leukemia (CML)

- ☐ Accelerated or blast phase
- ☐ Chronic phase
  - ☐ Bone marrow or stem cell transplantation performed
  - ☐ Progressive disease following initial anticancer therapy

Diagnostic Basis

☐ Bone marrow examination confirming acute leukemia or CML

☐ Chromosomal analysis confirming Philadelphia chromosome (if applicable)

☐ Peripheral blood, cerebrospinal fluid examination, or testicular biopsy confirming recurrence

☐ Other diagnostic methods consistent with current medical knowledge (please specify):

Treatment History

☐ Bone marrow or stem cell transplantation Date of transplantation: _______________

☐ Initial anticancer therapy Type: ___________________Date of initiation: _______________

☐ Other treatments (please specify):____

Current Disease Status

☐ In remission ☐ Relapsed (date of relapse: ____________________________________)

☐ Progressive disease ☐ Residual impairments (please specify):____________________

Functional Impairments and Residual Effects

☐ Neurological impairments ☐ Cardiopulmonary complications

☐ Immunosuppression-related issues

☐ Other organ system involvement (please specify): _____________________________________

Prognosis and Expected Recovery Timeline

☐ Expected recovery within 12 months ☐ Expected recovery within 24 months

☐ Indeterminate prognosis ☐ Permanent impairment anticipated

Physician's Name: ________________________Physician's Signature: ________________________

SSA-113.09-THYROID GLAND

Patient Name:______________________________ Date of Exam:__________

Diagnosis:______________________________ Date of Diagnosis: __________

☐ Anaplastic (undifferentiated) carcinoma

☐ Carcinoma with metastases beyond the regional lymph nodes, progressive despite radioactive iodine therapy

☐ Medullary carcinoma with metastases beyond the regional lymph nodes Confirmatory Diagnostic Tests (check all that apply and provide results):

☐ Biopsy: ______________________________

☐ Imaging (CT/MRI/PET Scan): ______________________________

☐ Ultrasound: ______________________________

☐ Thyroid Function Tests: ______________________________

☐ Other (please specify): ______________________________

Extent of Disease:

Evidence of metastasis?

☐ No ☐ Yes; if yes, locations: ______________________________

Has the carcinoma progressed despite radioactive iodine therapy? (if applicable)

☐ Yes ☐ No

Has the carcinoma metastasized beyond regional lymph nodes?

☐ Yes ☐ No

Treatment History:

Surgery:

☐ No ☐ Yes; type: ______________________________

Radiation Therapy:

☐ No ☐ Yes

Radioactive Iodine Therapy:

☐ No ☐ Yes

Chemotherapy or Targeted Therapy:

☐ No ☐ Yes; if yes, describe regimen and response: ______________________

Other treatments: ____

Functional Impairments and Symptoms (check all that apply):

☐ Significant weight loss ☐ Difficulty swallowing or breathing ☐ Fatigue

☐ Hoarseness or voice changes ☐ Pain or pressure in the neck

☐ Other (describe): ____

Prognosis and Additional Comments:

____

____

Physician's Name: ____________________ Physician's Signature: ____________________

SSA-113.12-RETINOBLASTOMA

Patient Name:____ Date of Exam:______________

Diagnosis: Retinoblastoma (Check all that apply)

Does the patient have retinoblastoma with extension beyond the orbit?

☐ Yes ☐ No

Has the patient experienced persistent or recurrent retinoblastoma following initial anticancer therapy?

☐ Yes ☐ No

Is there evidence of regional or distant metastases?

☐ Yes ☐ No

Additional Comments:

____

____

____

Physician's Name: __________________________Physician's Signature: __________________________

SSA-113.13-PRIMARY CENTRAL NERVOUS SYSTEM (CNS) CANCERS

Patient Name:______________________________________ Date of Exam:____________

Does the patient have a primary CNS cancer (brain or spinal cord)?

[] No [] Yes

Specify the type of CNS cancer diagnosed:

[] Glioblastoma multiforme [] ependymoblastoma [] diffuse intrinsic brain stem gliomas

[] astrocytoma [] sarcomas [] medulloblastoma

[] other primitive neuroectodermal tumors (PNETs):____________________________

WHO Classification of Tumors of the CNS (check one):

[] Grade I [] Grade II [] Grade III [] Grade IV

Is the tumor metastatic?

[] No [] Yes

Has the cancer progressed or recurred following initial anticancer therapy?

[] No [] Yes; If yes:

[] progressed:______________________________________

[] recurred: ______________________________________

What treatments has the patient received? (Check all that apply)

[] Surgery

[] crainiotomy [] spinal cord tumor resection

[] laser ablation/endoscopic surgery [] other:____________________________

[] Radiation Therapy

[] external beam radiation therapy (EBRT) [] stereotactic radiosurgery (SRS)

[] proton therapy [] other:______________________________________

[ ] Chemotherapy

[ ] temozolomide (TMZ)   [ ] carmustine (BCNU)

[ ] lomustine (CCNU)   [ ] methotrexate

[ ] bevacizumab   [ ] other:______________________________

[ ] Targeted Therapy & Immunotherapy

[ ] bevacizumab (Avastin)   [ ] BRAF inhibitors (dabrafenib, vemurafenib)

[ ] checkpoint inhibitors (penbrolizumab, nivolumab)   [ ] Tumor Treating Fields

[ ] Steriods & Supportive Care   Date of initial treatment: ____________

Has the cancer shown resistance or poor response to treatment?

[ ] No   [ ] Yes

Has the patient experienced any neurological or psychological impairments as a result of the CNS cancer?

[ ] No

[ ] Yes, if yes:

[ ] Neurological: ______________________________

[ ] Psychological: ______________________________

Describe complications (if any):______________________________

____

Describe any limitations in activities of daily living

[ ] mobility______________________________

____

[ ] self-care:______________________________

____

[ ] communication:______________________________

____

[ ] work activities:______________________________

____

Physician's Name: ____________________Physician's Signature: ____________________

SSA-113.21-NEUROBLASTOMA

Patient Name:______________________________________ Date of Exam:______________

Has Nauroblastoma been diagnosed:

[] No

[] Yes

Does the neuroblastoma extend across the midline?

☐ Yes

☐ No

Does the patient have distant metastases?

☐ Yes

☐ No

Has the neuroblastoma recurred after initial treatment?

☐ Yes

☐ No

Did the onset of neuroblastoma occur at age 1 year or older?

☐ Yes

☐ No

Please provide any additional relevant details regarding the patient's:

Neuroblastoma diagnosis:____

____

Treatment history: ____

____

Prognosis:____

____

Physician's Name: _________________________Physician's Signature: _________________________

SSA-113.29-MALIGNANT MELANOMA (SKIN, OCULAR OR MUCOSAL MELANOMAS)

Patient Name:____________________________________ Date of Exam:____________

Diagnosis of Malignant Melanoma:

☐ Skin melanoma

☐ Ocular melanoma

☐ Mucosal melanoma

[ ] Recurrent Disease (Select if applicable):

Has the patient experienced recurrence of melanoma? (Please note: an additional primary melanoma at a different site is not considered recurrent disease)

- ☐ No
- ☐ Yes; If yes, please specify:
  - ☐ Following wide excision (for skin melanoma)
  - ☐ Following enucleation of the eye (for ocular melanoma)

[ ] Metastatic Disease (Select if applicable):

- ☐ Metastases to one or more clinically apparent nodes (detected by imaging studies or clinical evaluation of palpable nodes)
- ☐ Metastases to four or more nodes that are not clinically apparent
- ☐ Metastases to adjacent skin (satellite lesions) or distant sites (e.g., liver, lung, or brain)

Has the patient been diagnosed with mucosal melanoma?

☐ Yes

☐ No

Please provide any additional relevant details regarding the patient's melanoma diagnosis, treatment history, or prognosis:____

____

____

____

Physician's Name: ____________________Physician's Signature: ____________________

SSA-114.02-SYSTEMIC LUPUS ERYTHEMATOSUS

Patient Name:____ Date of Exam:______________

Does the patient have a confirmed diagnosis of Systemic Lupus Erythematosus (SLE)?

[ ] No [ ] Yes; If yes, please provide the date of diagnosis: ______________________________

What diagnostic criteria were used? (Check all that apply)

[ ] 2019 EULAR/ACR [ ] 1998 ACR Criteria [ ] Other: ______________________

Does the patient have involvement of two or more organs/body systems due to SLE?

[ ] No [ ] Yes; If yes, indicate which organs/body systems are affected and describe severity:

____

Organ/SystemClinical FindingsSeverity Level (Mild/Moderate/Severe)

[ ] Respiratory (pleuritis, pneumonitis)

☐No Limitation ☐Mild ☐Moderate ☐Marked ☐Extreme

Clinical Findings____

[ ] Cardiovascular (endocarditis, myocarditis, pericarditis, vasculitis)

☐No Limitation ☐Mild ☐Moderate ☐Marked ☐Extreme

Clinical Findings____

[ ] Renal (glomerulonephritis)

☐No Limitation ☐Mild ☐Moderate ☐Marked ☐Extreme

Clinical Findings____

[ ] Hematologic (anemia, leukopenia, thrombocytopenia)

☐No Limitation ☐Mild ☐Moderate ☐Marked ☐Extreme

Clinical Findings____

[ ] Skin (photosensitivity)

☐No Limitation ☐Mild ☐Moderate ☐Marked ☐Extreme

Clinical Findings____

[ ] Neurologic (seizures)

☐No Limitation ☐Mild ☐Moderate ☐Marked ☐Extreme

Clinical Findings____

[ ] Mental (anxiety, cognition issues, mood disorders,psychosis)

☐No Limitation ☐Mild ☐Moderate ☐Marked ☐Extreme

Clinical Findings____

[ ] Immune System (inflammatory arthritis)

☐No Limitation ☐Mild ☐Moderate ☐Marked ☐Extreme

Clinical Findings____

[ ] Other (please specify):____________________________________

☐No Limitation ☐Mild ☐Moderate ☐Marked ☐Extreme

Clinical Findings____

Does at least one organ/system exhibit moderate or severe involvement?

[ ] No

[ ] Yes

Does the patient exhibit at least two of the following constitutional symptoms or signs?

[ ] No [ ] Yes; if yes check all that apply

[ ]severe fatigue [ ] fever [ ] malaise [ ] involuntary weight loss

[ ] Other:____

If yes, please describe the frequency and severity of these symptoms:____________________

____

Please indicate relevant laboratory test results confirming SLE

[] ANA   [] anti-dsDNA   [] complement levels   [] inflammatory markers

[] other:____

Does the patient experience limitations in activities of daily living (ADLs) due to SLE?

[] No   [] Yes; if so check all that apply:

[] Bathing   [] Dressing   [] Eating   [] Grooming

[] Toileting   [] Transferring   [] Mobility   [] Managing Finances

[] Meal Preparation   [] Housekeeping   [] Communication   ] Medication Management

[] Other____________________________   [] Using Transportation

Describe these limitations:____________________________________

____

What is your patient's current treatment regimen (check all that apply)

[] medications   [] therapies   [] lifestyle modifications

[] other:____

Has the patient responded adequately to treatment?

[] Yes   [] No; if no or partially, describe ongoing symptoms or complications:__________

____

Additional Comments: ____________________________________

____

Physician's Name: ____________________Physician's Signature: ____________________

SSA-114.03-SYSTEMIC VASCULITIS

Patient Name:____ Date of Exam:______________

Please confirm the patient's diagnosis of systemic vasculitis. If the diagnosis is confirmed, check the appropriate level of severity and organ involvement.

- ☐ Yes, diagnosis of systemic vasculitis is confirmed.
- ☐ No, diagnosis of systemic vasculitis is not confirmed.

Has the systemic vasculitis involved two or more organs or body systems? If so, please indicate which organs/systems are involved:

- ☐ Yes, two or more organs/systems involved.
- ☐ No, only one organ/system involved.

If yes, please indicate the organs/body systems involved:

Organs	Body Systems
[] Heart	[] Circulatory System
[] Lungs	[] Respiratory System
[] Kidneys	[] Digestive System
[] Liver	[] Nervous System
[] Brain	[] Muscular System
[] Stomach	[] Skeletal System
[] Intestines (Small & Large)	[] Endocrine System
[] Bladder	[] Urinary System
[] Pancreas	[] Lymphatic/Immune System
[] Skin	[] Reproductive System
	[] Integumentary System

Has one of the involved organs or body systems been affected to at least a moderate level of severity? Please provide details:

- ☐ Yes, at least one organ/body system is involved at a moderate level of severity.
- ☐ No, none of the organs/body systems are involved at a moderate level of severity.

Details regarding severity of involvement (including clinical signs and symptoms):

____

____

Please confirm if the patient is experiencing at least two of the following constitutional symptoms and signs associated with systemic vasculitis:

☐ Severe fatigue ☐ Fever ☐ Malaise ☐ Involuntary weight loss

Please indicate the severity and frequency of these symptoms:

____

____

Please provide any additional clinical information relevant to the patient's diagnosis of systemic vasculitis, including any associated conditions (e.g., autoimmune disorders such as SLE or dermatomyositis, or other forms of vasculitis such as Kawasaki disease or Henoch-Schonlein purpura):

____

____

Has the patient undergone angiography or tissue biopsy to confirm the diagnosis of systemic vasculitis? Please provide details of the diagnostic tests:

- ☐ Yes, angiography was performed.
- ☐ Yes, tissue biopsy was performed.
- ☐ No angiography or tissue biopsy was performed.

Please include any reports from the diagnostic procedures (angiography or biopsy) and any relevant findings:

____

____

Please provide any other relevant information regarding the patient's condition, treatment, or prognosis:

Condition: ____

____

Treatment: ____

____

Prognosis: ____

____

Physician's Name: ________________________ Physician's Signature: ________________________

SSA-114.04-SYSTEMIC SCLEROSIS (SCLERODERMA)

Patient Name:______________________________ Date of Exam:__________

Does the patient have a confirmed diagnosis of systemic sclerosis (scleroderma)?
[ ] No [ ] Yes; If yes; Date of Diagnosis: __________

What diagnostic methods were used? (Check all that apply):
[ ] clinical examination:______________________________
[ ] blood tests: ______________________________
[ ] nailfold capillaroscopy: ______________________________
[ ] imaging tests: ______________________________
[ ] pulmonary function tests: ______________________________
[ ] gastrointestinal tests: ______________________________
[ ] skin biopsy: ______________________________
[ ] other: ______________________________

Does the patient have involvement of two or more organs/body systems (check all that apply?

Organs	Body Systems
[ ] Heart	[ ] Circulatory System
[ ] Lungs	[ ] Respiratory System
[ ] Kidneys	[ ] Digestive System
[ ] Liver	[ ] Nervous System
[ ] Brain	[ ] Muscular System
[ ] Stomach	[ ] Skeletal System
[ ] Intestines (Small & Large)	[ ] Endocrine System
[ ] Bladder	[ ] Urinary System
[ ] Pancreas	[ ] Lymphatic/Immune System
[ ] Skin	[ ] Reproductive System
	[ ] Integumentary System

Has one of the involved organs or body systems been affected to at least a moderate level of severity?

- ☐ Yes, at least one organ/body system is involved at a moderate level of severity.
- ☐ No, none of the organs/body systems are involved at a moderate level of severity.

Details regarding severity of involvement (including clinical signs and symptoms):

____

____

Does the patient experience at least two of the following constitutional symptoms?(Check all that apply)

[] severe fatigue [] fever [] malaise [] involuntary weight loss

[] other: ______________________________

Does the patient have any toe contractures or fixed deformity of one or both feet?

[] No

[] Yes; If yes,

Does the patient have a documented medical need for (check all that apply):

[] a walker [] bilateral canes [] bilateral crutches

[] wheeled and seated mobility device involving the use of both hands

Does the patient have an inability to use one upper extremity to independently initiate, sustain, and complete age-appropriate activities involving fine and gross movements, and a documented medical need for (check all that apply):

[] a one-handed, hand-held assistive device that requires the use of the other upper extremity

[] a wheeled and seated mobility device involving the use of one hand

Does the patient have any finger contractures or fixed deformity in both hands?

[] No

[] Yes, if yes,

Does this prevent the patient from independently initiating, sustaining, and completing fine and gross motor activities?

[] No

[] Yes; If yes describe: ______________________________

____

Does the patient have atrophy with irreversible damage in one or both lower extremities?

[] No

[] Yes; If yes, does the patient have a documented medical need for (check all that apply):

[] a walker [] bilateral canes [] bilateral crutches

[] wheeled and seated mobility device involving the use of both hands

Does the patient have an inability to use one upper extremity to independently initiate, sustain, and complete age-appropriate activities involving fine and gross movements, and a documented medical need for (check all that apply):

[] a one-handed, hand-held assistive device that requires the use of the other upper extremity

[] a wheeled and seated mobility device involving the use of one hand

Does the patient have atrophy with irreversible damage in both upper extremities?

[] No

[] Yes; If yes,

Does this prevent the patient from independently initiating, sustaining, and completing fine and gross motor activities?

[] No

[] Yes, If yes describe: ______________________________

____

Does the patient have Raynaud's phenomenon with (check all that apply):

[] Gangrene involving at least two extremities?

[] Ischemia with ulcerations of toes or fingers?

If so, does the patient have a documented medical need for (check all that apply):

[] a walker [] bilateral canes [] bilateral crutches

[] wheeled and seated mobility device involving the use of both hands

Does the patient have an inability to use one upper extremity to independently initiate, sustain, and complete age-appropriate activities involving fine and gross movements, and a documented medical need for (check all that apply):

[] a one-handed, hand-held assistive device that requires the use of the other upper extremity

[] a wheeled and seated mobility device involving the use of one hand

Does the patient have an inability to use both upper extremities to the extent that neither can be used to independently initiate, sustain, and complete age-appropriate activities involving fine and gross movements?

[] Yes [] No

Additional Comments:

____

____

Physician's Name: ______________________ Physician's Signature: ______________________

SSA-114.05-POLYMYOSITIS AND DERMATOMYOSITIS

Patient Name:______________________________ Date of Exam:____________

Diagnosis:______________________________ Date of Diagnosis: ____________

Does the patient have proximal limb-girdle (pelvic or shoulder) muscle weakness?

[] No

[] Yes; If yes, please indicate which of the following applies (check all that apply):

Does the patient have a documented medical need for (check all that apply):

[] a walker [] bilateral canes [] bilateral crutches

[] wheeled and seated mobility device involving the use of both hands

Does the patient have an inability to use one upper extremity to independently initiate, sustain, and complete age-appropriate activities involving fine and gross movements, and a documented medical need for (check all that apply):

[] a one-handed, hand-held assistive device that requires the use of the other upper extremity

[] a wheeled and seated mobility device involving the use of one hand

Does the patient have an inability to use both upper extremities to the extent that neither can be used to independently initiate, sustain, and complete age-appropriate activities involving fine and gross movements?

[] Yes [] No

Does the patient have impaired swallowing with aspiration due to muscle weakness?

[] No [] Yes; If yes, please provide medical documentation and describe any interventions required: ______________________________

____

Does the patient have impaired respiration due to intercostal and diaphragmatic muscle weakness?

[] No

[] Yes; If yes, please provide medical documentation and indicate any interventions required such as (check all that apply:

[] ventilatory support [] , oxygen therapy) [] other: ______________

Does the patient have diffuse calcinosis with limitation of joint mobility or intestinal motility?

[] No [] Yes; If yes, please describe the extent of joint mobility or intestinal motility limitation: ______________________________

____

Additional Comments: ______________________________

____

Physician's Name: ______________ Physician's Signature: ______________

SSA-114.06-UNDIFFERENTIATED AND MIXED CONNECTIVE TISSUE DISEASE

Patient Name:______________________________________ Date of Exam:____________

Diagnosis: Undifferentiated and Mixed Connective Tissue Disease (MCTD)

Does the patient have involvement of two or more organs/body systems?
[] No
[] Yes; If yes, please specify the affected organs/body systems and describe the severity of each:

Organs	Body Systems
[] Heart	[] Circulatory System
[] Lungs	[] Respiratory System
[] Kidneys	[] Digestive System
[] Liver	[] Nervous System
[] Brain	[] Muscular System
[] Stomach	[] Skeletal System
[] Intestines (Small & Large)	[] Endocrine System
[] Bladder	[] Urinary System
[] Pancreas	[] Lymphatic/Immune System
[] Skin	[] Reproductive System
	[] Integumentary System

Has one of the involved organs or body systems been affected to at least a moderate level of severity?

- [] Yes, at least one organ/body system is involved at a moderate level of severity.
- [] No, none of the organs/body systems are involved at a moderate level of severity.

Details regarding severity of involvement (including clinical signs and symptoms):

____

____

At least one organ/body system must be affected at a moderate level of severity. Does the patient meet this criterion?
[] No [] Yes

Does the patient have at least two of the following symptoms? (Check all that apply)
[] severe fatigue [] fever [] malaise [] involuntary weight loss

Additional Comments: ____

____

Physician's Name: ______________________ Physician's Signature: ______________________

SSA-114.07-DEFICIENCY DISORDERS (EXCLUDING HIV INFECTION)

Patient Name:______________________________ Date of Exam:__________

Does the patient have a diagnosed immune deficiency disorder (excluding HIV infection)?

☐ No ☐ Yes; If yes, specify diagnosis: ______________________________

Has the patient experienced one or more of the following infections that are either resistant to treatment or required hospitalization or intravenous treatment three or more times in a 12-month period (check all that apply)?

[ ] Sepsis

Date of occurance:__________ Did it require [ ] Hospitalization [ ] IV treatment

[ ] Meningitis

Date of occurance:__________ Did it require [ ] Hospitalization [ ] IV treatment

[ ] Pneumonia

Date of occurance:__________ Did it require [ ] Hospitalization [ ] IV treatment

[ ] Septic Arthritis

Date of occurance:__________ Did it require [ ] Hospitalization [ ] IV treatment

[ ] Endocarditis

Date of occurance:__________ Did it require [ ] Hospitalization [ ] IV treatment

[ ] Sinusitis (documented by imaging)

Date of occurance:__________ Did it require [ ] Hospitalization [ ] IV treatment

Has the patient undergone a stem cell transplantation?

☐ No ☐ Yes; If yes, date of transplantation: ______________________________

Has it been at least 12 months since transplantation?

☐ No ☐ Yes, if yes, describe any residual impairments: ______________________________

____

Does the patient have any other complications or residual impairments related to their immune deficiency disorder?

☐ No ☐ Yes; if yes, please describe: ______________________________

____

Physician's Name: __________________Physician's Signature: __________________

SSA-114.09-INFLAMMATORY ARTHRITIS

Patient Name:____ Date of Exam:______________

Diagnosis: ____

Does the patient have persistent inflammation or deformity in one or more major joints of a lower extremity?

[] No

[] Yes; if yes, is there medical documentation of at least one of the following? (Check all that apply)

[] a walker [] bilateral canes [] bilateral crutches

[] wheeled and seated mobility device involving the use of both hands

Does the patient have an inability to use one upper extremity to independently initiate, sustain, and complete age-appropriate activities involving fine and gross movements, and a documented medical need for (check all that apply):

[] a one-handed, hand-held assistive device that requires the use of the other upper extremity

[] a wheeled and seated mobility device involving the use of one hand

Does the patient have persistent inflammation or deformity in one or more major joints in each upper extremity?

[] No [ ] Yes, if yes, is there medical documentation of an inability to use both upper extremities to the extent that neither can be used to independently initiate, sustain, and complete age-appropriate activities involving fine and gross movements?

[] No [] Yes

Does the patient have inflammation or deformity in one or more major joints of an upper or lower extremity?

[] No

[] Yes; if yes, is there involvement of two or more organs/body systems? (check all that apply):

Organs	Body Systems
[] Heart	[] Circulatory System
[] Lungs	[] Respiratory System
[] Kidneys	[] Digestive System
[] Liver	[] Nervous System
[] Brain	[] Muscular System
[] Stomach	[] Skeletal System
[] Intestines (Small & Large)	[] Endocrine System
[] Bladder	[] Urinary System
[] Pancreas	[] Lymphatic/Immune System
[] Skin	[] Reproductive System
	[] Integumentary System

Has one of the involved organs or body systems been affected to at least a moderate level of severity?

- ☐ Yes, at least one organ/body system is involved at a moderate level of severity.
- ☐ No, none of the organs/body systems are involved at a moderate level of severity.

If YES, does the patient exhibit at least two of the following constitutional symptoms or signs? (Check all that apply)

[] severe fatigue [] fever [] malaise [] involuntary weight loss

[] other: ______________________________

Does the patient have (check all that apply)?:

[] ankylosing spondylitis [] another spondyloarthropathy: ______________

If so, does the patient have ankylosis (fixation) of the dorsolumbar or cervical spine as shown by appropriate medically acceptable imaging?

[] No

[ ] Yes; if yes, what is the measured degree of flexion from the vertical position (zero degrees)?______________________________

____

Physician's Name: ______________Physician's Signature: ______________

SSA-114.10-SJöGREN'S SYNDROME

Patient Name:________________________________ Date of Exam:____________

Does the patient have a confirmed diagnosis of Sjögren's syndrome?

☐ No ☐ Yes; If yes, please provide the date of diagnosis: ____________________

Does the patient have involvement of two or more organs or body systems?

☐ No

☐ Yes; if yes, please indicate the affected organs/body systems and describe the severity:

Organs	Body Systems
[ ] Heart	[ ] Circulatory System
[ ] Lungs	[ ] Respiratory System
[ ] Kidneys	[ ] Digestive System
[ ] Liver	[ ] Nervous System
[ ] Brain	[ ] Muscular System
[ ] Stomach	[ ] Skeletal System
[ ] Intestines (Small & Large)	[ ] Endocrine System
[ ] Bladder	[ ] Urinary System
[ ] Pancreas	[ ] Lymphatic/Immune System
[ ] Skin	[ ] Reproductive System
	[ ] Integumentary System

Has one of the involved organs or body systems been affected to at least a moderate level of severity?

- ☐ Yes, at least one organ/body system is involved at a moderate level of severity.
- ☐ No, none of the organs/body systems are involved at a moderate level of severity.

Does the patient exhibit at least two of the following constitutional symptoms (check all that apply)?

[ ] Severe fatigue [ ] Fever [ ] Malaise [ ] Involuntary weight loss

Please describe any relevant laboratory findings, imaging results, or other diagnostic evidence supporting this assessment:____

____

Physician's Name: ____________________ Physician's Signature: ____________________

SSA-114.11-HUMAN IMMUNODEFICIENCY VIRUS (HIV) INFECTION

Patient Name:______________________________________ Date of Exam:______________

Does the patient have a confirmed diagnosis of HIV infection?
[] No [] Yes

Check all applicable conditions related to the patient's HIV infection:
[] opportunistic infections (OIs): ____
[] HIV-Related Malignancies: ____
[] Neurological Disorders: ____
[] Other HIV-Related Conditions: ____

Immune System MarkersCD4 Count or Percentage (114.00F4) (check all that apply):
[] child from birth to attainment of age 1:
- [] absolute CD4 count of 500 cells/mm3 or less
- [] CD4 percentage of less than 15 percent
- [] other:____

[] children from age 1 to attainment of age 5:
- [] absolute CD4 count of 200 cells/mm3 or less
- [] CD4 percentage of less than 15 percent
- [] other: ____

[] child from age 5 to attainment of age 18:
- [] absolute CD4 count of 50 cells/mm3 or less
- [] other: ____

Has the patient experienced?:
[] complications of HIV
[] requiring at least three hospitalizations within a 12-month period, at least 30 days apart, each lasting at least 48 hours?

Date of Hospitalization	Hours Hospitalized:
Date of Hospitalization	Hours Hospitalized:
Date of Hospitalization	Hours Hospitalized:
Date of Hospitalization	Hours Hospitalized:

Does the patient have any of the following HIV-related neurological manifestations? Check all that apply:

[ ] impaired brain growth [ ] brain atrophy documented by CT scan or MRI
[ ] developmental regression [ ] loss of acquired intellectual abilities
[ ] forgetting information previously learned [ ] inability to learn new information
[ ] sudden onset of new learning disability [ ] developmental delay without regression

Does the patient meet the criteria for immune suppression and growth failure?

[ ] No [ ] Yes

CD4 Measurement:

[ ] child from birth to attainment of age 5
  [ ] CD4 percentage of less than 20 percent

[ ] child from age 5 to attainment of age 18
  [ ] absolute CD4 count of less than 200 cells/mm3
  [ ] CD4 percentage of less than 14 percent

Growth Failure (Choose One):

[ ] child from birth to age 2:

Are there three weight-for-length measurements that meet the following criteria?

Within a consecutive 12-month period At least 60 days apart .

Less than the third percentile on the appropriate weight-for-length table under 105.08B1

[ ] No [ ] Yes

If Yes, please provide measurement dates and percentiles:

Date 1: ________________ Percentile: _____________%

Date 2: ________________ Percentile: _____________%

Date 3: ________________ Percentile: _____________%

[ ] child age 2 to 18:Are there three BMI-for-age measurements that meet the following criteria?

Within a consecutive 12-month period At least 60 days apart .

Less than the third percentile on the appropriate BMI-for-age table under 105.08B2

[ ] No [ ] Yes

If Yes, please provide measurement dates and percentiles:

Date 1: ________________ BMI Percentile: _________%

Date 2: ________________ BMI Percentile: _________%

Date 3: ________________ BMI Percentile: _________%

Physician's Name: ________________________Physician's Signature: ________________________

Table 1 - Grading System of Muscle Function

Grade		Function of the Muscle
0	None	No visible or palpable contraction.
1	Trace	Visible or palpable contraction with no motion.
2	Poor	Active ROM with gravity eliminated.
3	Fair	Active ROM against gravity only, without resistance.
4	Good	Active ROM against gravity, moderate resistance.
5	Normal	Active ROM against gravity, maximum resistance.

102-SPECIAL SENSES & SPEECH

Table 1 - Visual Acuity Efficiency

Snellen best-corrected central visual acuity for distance		Visual acuity efficiency (%) (102.04A)
English	Metric	
20/16	6/5	100
20/20	6/6	100
20/25	6/7.5	95
20/30	6/9	90
20/40	6/12	85
20/50	6/15	75
20/60	6/18	70
20/70	6/21	65
20/80	6/24	60
20/100	6/30	50

Figure 1:

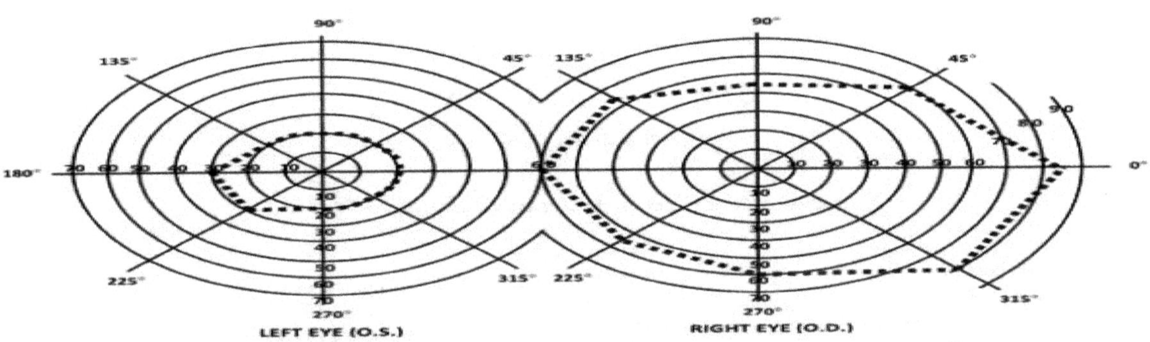

Table 2 - Visual Acuity Impairment Value

Snellen best-corrected central visual acuity for distance		Visual acuity impairment value (102.04B)
English	Metric	
20/16	6/5	0.00
20/20	6/6	0.00
20/25	6/7.5	0.10
20/30	6/9	0.18
20/40	6/12	0.30
20/50	6/15	0.40
20/60	6/18	0.48
20/70	6/21	0.54
20/80	6/24	0.60
20/100	6/30	0.70

103-RESPIRATORY DISORDERS

Table I: FEV_1 Criteria for 103.02A

Table I-A		
Age 6 to attainment of age 13 (For both females and males)		
Height without shoes *(centimeters)* < means *less than*	Height without shoes *(inches)* < means *less than*	FEV_1 less than or equal to (L, BTPS)
<123.0	<48.50	0.80
123.0 to <129.0	48.50 to <50.75	0.90
129.0 to <134.0	50.75 to <52.75	1.00
134.0 to <139.0	52.75 to <54.75	1.10
139.0 to <144.0	54.75 to <56.75	1.20
144.0 to <149.0	56.75 to <58.75	1.30
149.0 or more	58.75 or more	1.40

Table I-B			
Age 13 to attainment of age 18			
Height without shoes *(centimeters)* < means *less than*	Height without shoes *(inches)* < means *less than*	*Females* FEV_1 less than or equal to (L, BTPS)	*Males* FEV_1 less than or equal to (L, BTPS)
<153.0	<60.25	1.35	1.40
153.0 to <159.0	60.25 to <62.50	1.45	1.50
159.0 to <164.0	62.50 to <64.50	1.55	1.60
164.0 to <169.0	64.50 to <66.50	1.65	1.70
169.0 to <174.0	66.50 to <68.50	1.75	1.85
174.0 to <180.0	68.50 to <70.75	1.85	2.00
180.0 or more	70.75 or more	1.95	2.10

Table II: FVC Criteria for 103.02B

Table II-A

Age 6 to attainment of age 13
(For both females and males)

Height without shoes *(centimeters)* < means *less than*	Height without shoes *(inches)* < means *less than*	FVC less than or equal to (L, BTPS)
<123.0	<48.50	0.85
123.0 to <129.0	48.50 to <50.75	1.00
129.0 to <134.0	50.75 to <52.75	1.10
134.0 to <139.0	52.75 to <54.75	1.30
139.0 to <144.0	54.75 to <56.75	1.40
144.0 to <149.0	56.75 to <58.75	1.55
149.0 or more	58.75 or more	1.70

Table II-B

Age 13 to attainment of age 18

Height without shoes *(centimeters)* < means *less than*	Height without shoes *(inches)* < means *less than*	*Females* FVC less than or equal to (L, BTPS)	*Males* FVC less than or equal to (L, BTPS)
<153.0	<60.25	1.65	1.65
153.0 to <159.0	60.25 to <62.50	1.70	1.80
159.0 to <164.0	62.50 to <64.50	1.80	1.95
164.0 to <169.0	64.50 to <66.50	1.95	2.10
169.0 to <174.0	66.50 to <68.50	2.05	2.25
174.0 to <180.0	68.50 to <70.75	2.20	2.45
180.0 or more	70.75 or more	2.30	2.55

Table III: FEV_1 Criteria for 103.04A

Table III-A		
Age 6 to attainment of age 13 (For both females and males)		
Height without shoes *(centimeters)* < means *less than*	Height without shoes *(inches)* < means *less than*	FEV_1 less than or equal to (L, BTPS)
<123.0	<48.50	1.00
123.0 to <129.0	48.50 to <50.75	1.15
129.0 to <134.0	50.75 to <52.75	1.25
134.0 to <139.0	52.75 to <54.75	1.40
139.0 to <144.0	54.75 to <56.75	1.50
144.0 to <149.0	56.75 to <58.75	1.70
149.0 or more	58.75 or more	1.80

Table III-B			
Age 13 to attainment of age 18			
Height without shoes *(centimeters)* < means *less than*	Height without shoes *(inches)* < means *less than*	*Females* FEV_1 less than or equal to (L, BTPS)	*Males* FEV_1 less than or equal to (L, BTPS)
<153.0	<60.25	1.75	1.85
153.0 to <159.0	60.25 to <62.50	1.85	2.05
159.0 to <164.0	62.50 to <64.50	1.95	2.15
164.0 to <169.0	64.50 to <66.50	2.10	2.30
169.0 to <174.0	66.50 to <68.50	2.25	2.45
174.0 to <180.0	68.50 to <70.75	2.35	2.60
180.0 or more	70.75 or more	2.50	2.70

104-CARDIOVASCULAR SYSTEM

Table I - Tachycardia at Rest

Age	Apical heart rate (beats per minute)
Under 1 year	150
1 through 3 years	130
4 through 9 years	120
10 through 15 years	110
Over 15 years	100

Table II - Tachypnea at Rest

Age	Respiratory rate over (per minute)
Under 1 year	40
1 through 5 years	35
6 through 9 years	30
Over 9 years	25

Third Percentile Values for Weight-for Length		
Length (Centimeters)	Weight (kilograms)	
	Table I – Males Birth to Attainment of Age 2	Table II – Females Birth to Attainment of Age 2
45.0	1.597	1.613
45.5	1.703	1.724
46.5	1.919	1.946
47.5	2.139	2.171
48.5	2.364	2.397
49.5	2.592	2.624
50.5	2.824	2.852
51.5	3.058	3.081
52.5	3.294	3.310
53.5	3.532	3.538
54.5	3.771	3.767
55.5	4.010	3.994
56.5	4.250	4.220
57.5	4.489	4.445
58.5	4.728	4.669
59.5	4.966	4.892
60.5	5.203	5.113
61.5	5.438	5.333
62.5	5.671	5.552
63.5	5.903	5.769
64.5	6.132	5.985
65.5	6.359	6.200
66.5	6.584	6.413
67.5	6.807	6.625
68.5	7.027	6.836
69.5	7.245	7.046
70.5	7.461	7.254

71.5	7.674	7.461
72.5	7.885	7.667
73.5	8.094	7.871
74.5	8.301	8.075
75.5	8.507	8.277
76.5	8.710	8.479
77.5	8.913	8.679
78.5	9.113	8.879
79.5	9.313	9.078
80.5	9.512	9.277
81.5	9.710	9.476
82.5	9.907	9.674
83.5	10.104	9.872
84.5	10.301	10.071
85.5	10.499	10.270
86.5	10.696	10.469
87.5	10.895	10.670
88.5	11.095	10.871
89.5	11.296	11.074
90.5	11.498	11.278
91.5	11.703	11.484
92.5	11.910	11.691
93.5	12.119	11.901
94.5	12.331	12.112
95.5	12.546	12.326
96.5	12.764	12.541
97.5	12.987	12.760
98.5	13.213	12.981
99.5	13.443	13.205
100.5	13.678	13.431
101.5	13.918	13.661
102.5	14.163	13.895
103.5	14.413	14.132

Third Percentile Values for BMI-for-Age			
Table III – Males Age 2 to Attainment of Age 18		**Table IV – Females Age 2 to Attainment of Age 18**	
Age (yrs. and mos.)	**BMI**	**Age (yrs. and mos.)**	**BMI**
2.0 to 2.1	14.5	2.0 to 2.2	14.1
2.2 to 2.4	14.4	2.3 to 2.6	14.0
2.5 to 2.7	14.3	2.7 to 2.10	13.9
2.8 to 2.11	14.2	2.11 to 3.2	13.8
3.0 to 3.2	14.1	3.3 to 3.6	13.7
3.3 to 3.6	14.0	3.7 to 3.11	13.6
3.7 to 3.11	13.9	4.0 to 4.4	13.5
4.0 to 4.5	13.8	4.5 to 4.11	13.4
4.6 to 5.0	13.7	5.0 to 5.9	13.3
5.1 to 6.0	13.6	5.10 to 7.6	13.2
6.1 to 7.6	13.5	7.7 to 8.4	13.3
7.7 to 8.6	13.6	8.5 to 8.10	13.4
8.7 to 9.1	13.7	8.11 to 9.3	13.5
9.2 to 9.6	13.8	9.4 to 9.8	13.6
9.7 to 9.11	13.9	9.9 to 10.0	13.7
10.0 to 10.3	14.0	10.1 to 10.4	13.8
10.4 to 10.7	14.1	10.5 to 10.7	13.9
10.8 to 10.10	14.2	10.8 to 10.10	14.0
10.11 to 11.2	14.3	10.11 to 11.2	14.1
11.3 to 11.5	14.4	11.3 to 11.5	14.2
11.6 to 11.8	14.5	11.6 to 11.7	14.3
11.9 to 11.11	14.6	11.8 to 11.10	14.4
12.0 to 12.1	14.7	11.11 to 12.1	14.5
12.2 to 12.4	14.8	12.2 to 12.4	14.6
12.5 to 12.7	14.9	12.5 to 12.6	14.7
12.8 to 12.9	15.0	12.7 to 12.9	14.8

12.10 to 13.0	15.1	12.10 to 12.11	14.9
13.1 to 13.2	15.2	13.0 to 13.2	15.0
13.3 to 13.4	15.3	13.3 to 13.4	15.1
13.5 to 13.7	15.4	13.5 to 13.7	15.2
13.8 to 13.9	15.5	13.8 to 13.9	15.3
13.10 to 13.11	15.6	13.10 to 14.0	15.4
14.0 to 14.1	15.7	14.1 to 14.2	15.5
14.2 to 14.4	15.8	14.3 to 14.5	15.6
14.5 to 14.6	15.9	14.6 to 14.7	15.7
14.7 to 14.8	16.0	14.8 to 14.9	15.8
14.9 to 14.10	16.1	14.10 to 15.0	15.9
14.11 to 15.0	16.2	15.1 to 15.2	16.0
15.1 to 15.3	16.3	15.3 to 15.5	16.1
15.4 to 15.5	16.4	15.6 to 15.7	16.2
15.6 to 15.7	16.5	15.8 to 15.10	16.3
15.8 to 15.9	16.6	15.11 to 16.0	16.4
15.10 to 15.11	16.7	16.1 to 16.3	16.5
16.0 to 16.1	16.8	16.4 to 16.6	16.6
16.2 to 16.3	16.9	16.7 to 16.9	16.7
16.4 to 16.5	17.0	16.10 to 17.0	16.8
16.6 to 16.8	17.1	17.1 to 17.3	16.9
16.9 to 16.10	17.2	17.4 to 17.7	17.0
16.11 to 17.0	17.3	17.8 to 17.11	17.1
17.1 to 17.2	17.4		
17.3 to 17.5	17.5		
17.6 to 17.7	17.6		
17.8 to 17.9	17.7		
17.10 to 17.11	17.8		

A

Ability to Work-Refers to a claimant's capacity to engage in substantial gainful activity (SGA) on a sustained basis. The Social Security Administration (SSA) evaluates both physical and mental limitations to determine whether an individual can perform past relevant work or adjust to other work in the national economy.

Activities of Daily Living (ADLs)-Fundamental personal tasks such as eating, bathing, dressing, grooming, using the toilet, and managing basic household responsibilities. SSA assesses how impairments interfere with a claimant's ability to perform ADLs when evaluating functional limitations.

Administrative Law Judge (ALJ)-A federal judge employed by the SSA's Office of Hearings Operations (OHO). ALJs conduct disability hearings, take testimony, consider evidence, and issue written decisions regarding eligibility for disability benefits.

Alleged Onset Date (AOD)-The date the claimant asserts that their disabling condition began. This date is established by the applicant and is later evaluated by SSA to determine the official Established Onset Date (EOD) based on medical and vocational evidence.

Amended Onset Date-A new onset date proposed or agreed upon by the claimant, often during a hearing, to align better with the medical evidence or procedural requirements. Acceptance of an amended onset date may expedite approval or increase benefit eligibility.

Appeal-A formal request for SSA to review and reconsider a denied claim. The four levels of appeal include:1-Reconsideration; 2-Hearing by an ALJ; 3-Review by the Appeals Council; 4-Federal court review

Appeals Council-A division of SSA located in Falls Church, Virginia, that reviews decisions made by ALJs upon request. The Council may uphold, reverse, remand, or dismiss the ALJ's decision.

Applicant-An individual who files for Social Security Disability Insurance (SSDI) or Supplemental Security Income (SSI) benefits. The applicant may also be referred to as the claimant.

Application Date-The date on which a completed disability application is filed with SSA. It is important because it affects the onset and retroactive benefit periods.

Appropriate Medical Treatment-Treatment consistent with accepted medical standards for a given condition. SSA assesses whether a claimant is receiving appropriate care and whether noncompliance is justified by the impairment itself.

Assistive Devices-Medical or mobility aids, such as walkers, crutches, canes, wheelchairs, prosthetics, or hearing aids, that help individuals perform daily activities. SSA considers the use and necessity of these devices when evaluating the severity of an impairment.

Asymptomatic-A medical condition that does not present observable symptoms. SSA typically requires both diagnosis and functional limitations, so asymptomatic conditions may not qualify as disabling without evidence of significant functional impact.

Attending Physician-A healthcare provider with an ongoing treatment relationship with the claimant. SSA gives weight to the medical opinions of treating sources, especially if their assessments are well-supported by objective medical evidence.

Axis I/Axis II Diagnoses-Terms used in previous versions of the Diagnostic and Statistical Manual of Mental Disorders (DSM). Axis I included clinical psychiatric disorders; Axis II included personality disorders and intellectual disabilities. While SSA now references the updated DSM-5, legacy terms may still appear in medical records.

B

Back Pay: Retroactive disability benefits paid to a claimant for the period between the established onset date of disability and the date the claim is approved. This may include benefits for up to 12 months prior to the application date, depending on when the disability began and when the claim was filed.

Beneficiary: A person who receives Social Security or Supplemental Security Income (SSI) benefits. In the context of disability, this usually refers to someone approved for Social Security Disability Insurance (SSDI) or SSI.

Benefit Verification Letter: A letter from the SSA that provides proof of a person's Social Security benefits, including the type, amount, and start date of benefits received.

Blindness (Statutory): A condition defined by the SSA as central visual acuity of 20/200 or less in the better eye with the use of a correcting lens, or a visual field limitation such that the widest diameter of the visual field subtends an angle no greater than 20 degrees. Different rules and income limits may apply to blind individuals.

Blue Book: An informal name for the Disability Evaluation Under Social Security, the SSA's medical guide that outlines the criteria used to determine whether an individual's condition meets a listed impairment.

Board-Certified: Refers to a medical doctor who has passed rigorous exams in a specialized field of medicine. SSA may give more weight to opinions of board-certified specialists in disability determinations.

Break in Benefits: A temporary cessation of disability benefits, often due to medical improvement, incarceration, or exceeding income/resource limits. Benefits may be reinstated if eligibility is re-established.

Burden of Proof: The obligation to present evidence to support a claim. In SSA disability cases, the claimant initially has the burden of proving that they are disabled under SSA's rules.

C

Calendar Quarter: A three-month period used by SSA to determine earnings and eligibility (e.g., Jan–Mar, Apr–Jun).

Capable of Performing Past Relevant Work: A determination that a claimant can do work they performed in the past 15 years, potentially leading to denial of disability benefits.

Cardiac Impairment: A condition affecting the heart (e.g., coronary artery disease, congestive heart failure) that may meet a listing under the cardiovascular system impairments.

Caregiver Statement: A form or letter completed by someone who regularly assists the claimant, describing functional limitations.

Childhood Disability: Refers to disability benefits or SSI for individuals under age 18, evaluated using different criteria than for adults.

Claim: An application for Social Security Disability Insurance (SSDI) or Supplemental Security Income (SSI).

Claimant: The person applying for disability benefits.

Closed Period of Disability: A claim for a specific past period during which the person was disabled but has since medically improved.

Commissioner of Social Security: The head of the Social Security Administration.

Common Law Marriage: A non-ceremonial marriage that may be recognized for survivor or spousal benefits in certain states.

Compassionate Allowances (CAL): A program that fast-tracks approval for claims involving specific, severe medical conditions.

Consultative Examination (CE): A medical exam arranged and paid for by SSA when more evidence is needed to decide a claim.

Continuing Disability Review (CDR): A periodic review to determine if a person still meets SSA's disability criteria.

Conversion: Changing from one type of benefit to another (e.g., from SSDI to retirement at full retirement age).
Coronary Artery Disease (CAD): A heart condition that may qualify under SSA's cardiovascular listings.
Cost of Living Adjustment (COLA): Annual increase in benefits to account for inflation.
Creditable Earnings: Wages or self-employment income on which SSA taxes were paid, used to determine eligibility for benefits.
Current Work Activity: Employment or self-employment evaluated under SSA's Substantial Gainful Activity (SGA) rules.
Custodial Parent: May be relevant in child SSI claims, where the child's household income is deemed from the parent(s).

D

Date Last Insured (DLI): The last date a person meets the earnings requirements for Social Security
Decision Notice A written document from the SSA explaining the outcome of a disability claim—either an approval or a denial—and the reasons behind the decision.
Denial: An official SSA decision that a claimant does not qualify for disability benefits, typically because they do not meet medical or non-medical eligibility criteria.
Development: The phase in the claims process during which SSA gathers medical, educational, and vocational evidence to evaluate disability claims.
Disability: For SSA purposes, the inability to engage in Substantial Gainful Activity (SGA) due to a medically determinable physical or mental impairment expected to last at least 12 months or result in death.
Disability Determination Services (DDS): State agencies that work with the SSA to review medical evidence and make initial decisions on disability claims.
Disability Hearing Officer (DHO): A specially trained SSA employee who conducts hearings for certain reconsideration-level appeals, especially for continuing disability reviews (CDRs).
Disability Insurance (SSDI): You must prove you became disabled before this date to qualify for SSDI.
Disability Insurance Benefits (DIB): Another term for SSDI—monthly benefits paid to people who have worked and paid into Social Security but can no longer work due to a disability.
Disabled Adult Child (DAC) A benefit category for adult children with disabilities that began before age 22, allowing them to receive SSDI based on a parent's Social Security record.
Disabled Widow(er)'s Benefits (DWB): Benefits available to a widow or widower over age 50 who becomes disabled within seven years of their spouse's death, based on the deceased spouse's earnings.
Duration Requirement: The rule that a disabling condition must be expected to last at least 12 continuous months or result in death.

E

Early Onset-Refers to disability that begins at an early age, often used in the context of diseases like early-onset Alzheimer's.
Earned Income-Income received from work (wages, salaries, self-employment). Affects SSI eligibility and benefit amount
Earned Income Exclusion-SSA disregards a portion of earned income when determining SSI benefits. The first $65 of earned income plus half the remainder is excluded.
Earnings Record-A detailed record of a worker's taxable earnings maintained by SSA. Used to calculate SSDI benefits.
Earnings Test-SSA test to determine how much a person can earn and still receive full Social Security benefits (typically applies to retirement, but also relevant in SSDI trial work periods).
Education and Work Experience-Factors SSA uses in determining residual functional capacity and ability to engage in substantial gainful activity (SGA).

Electronic Disability Collect System (EDCS)-An SSA system used to electronically process and store disability claims.
Electronic Records Express (ERE)-A secure SSA system that allows medical providers, representatives, and schools to submit records electronically.
Eligibility-General term referring to whether a claimant meets the requirements for benefits (e.g., work history, medical condition, income/resource limits).
Emergency Advance Payment-One-time immediate payment that may be made to an SSI applicant facing a financial emergency while waiting for benefits.
Employment Network (EN)-An organization that provides employment services to disability beneficiaries under the Ticket to Work program.
Epilepsy-A medical condition listed in SSA's Blue Book (Listing of Impairments), under Neurological Disorders.
Equitable Relief-SSA may use equitable relief provisions to correct administrative errors affecting benefit payments.
Essential Person-In some cases (particularly old SSI rules), a person whose presence is essential to the care of an SSI recipient.
Ex Parte Reopening-SSA may reopen a prior claim without a request if it benefits the claimant, under certain conditions.
Expedited Reinstatement (EXR)-Allows former disability beneficiaries to have benefits reinstated without a new application if their disability recurs within 5 years of termination due to work.
Extended Period of Eligibility (EPE)-A 36-month period after the Trial Work Period during which SSDI benefits can restart if the person stops working or earns below SGA.
Extra Help-A Medicare program (administered by SSA) that helps pay for Medicare Part D prescription drug costs for low-income individuals.

F

Fair Hearing – A legal process that allows a claimant to challenge decisions made by the SSA, particularly for SSI or Medicaid eligibility.
Family Maximum Benefit – The maximum total monthly benefit that can be paid to a family on a single worker's Social Security record.
Federal Benefit Rate (FBR) – The maximum monthly SSI payment set by the federal government before any state supplements or deductions.
Fee Agreement – A written agreement between a claimant and a representative (e.g., attorney) that outlines the payment for representation, subject to SSA approval.
Fee Petition – An alternative method for a representative to request payment for services, used when no fee agreement exists.
Field Office – Local SSA offices where individuals can apply for benefits, report changes, or get help with SSA services.
Five-Month Waiting Period – A mandatory period before SSDI benefits begin, starting from the established onset date of disability.
Form SSA-827 – "Authorization to Disclose Information to the Social Security Administration" – a consent form allowing SSA to obtain medical and other records.
Functional Capacity Evaluation (FCE) – A comprehensive assessment used to determine an individual's physical and/or mental ability to perform work-related tasks.
Functional Limitations – Restrictions in an individual's ability to perform basic work-related activities due to a medically determinable impairment.
Fully Favorable Decision – A decision by an Administrative Law Judge (ALJ) that grants all of the benefits requested, including the alleged onset date.
Fully Insured Status – A requirement for Social Security benefits based on the number of work credits earned over a person's working life.

G

Gainful Activity – See *Substantial Gainful Activity (SGA).* Refers to work activity that involves doing significant physical or mental activities for pay or profit. SSA evaluates this to determine disability status.

Garnishment – The legal withholding of a portion of a person's benefits (e.g., SSDI) to pay for debts like child support or federal student loans. Note: SSI benefits cannot be garnished in most cases.

Gastrointestinal Disorders – Medical impairments evaluated under SSA Listing 5.00. Includes conditions like Crohn's disease, IBS, and liver disorders.

General Assistance (GA) – A state or local government welfare program providing basic support to individuals who do not qualify for federal benefits like SSI or SSDI.

Genetic Disorders – May be evaluated under different listings depending on how they affect bodily systems (e.g., cystic fibrosis, Huntington's disease, or muscular dystrophy).

Global Assessment of Functioning (GAF) – A numerical scale (0 through 100) used by mental health professionals to rate a person's social, occupational, and psychological functioning. Although no longer in the DSM-5, it may still appear in older SSA records.

Guardian (Representative Payee) – A person or organization appointed to manage SSA benefits on behalf of someone unable to do so themselves, such as a child or adult with a disability.

Grid Rules (Medical-Vocational Guidelines) – A framework SSA uses to determine disability based on a combination of age, education, work experience, and functional capacity.

H

HALLEX (Hearings, Appeals and Litigation Law Manual)-The SSA's internal manual used by the Office of Hearings Operations to guide ALJs and staff in handling hearings and appeals.

Headache Disorders-A category of medical impairments (like migraines or cluster headaches) that may be considered under SSA listings or evaluated for functional limitations.

Hearing (Administrative Hearing)-A formal proceeding before an Administrative Law Judge (ALJ) where disability claimants can present evidence and testimony supporting their case.

Hearing Impairment-A medically determinable condition that can qualify for disability benefits under SSA Listing 2.10 or 2.11, depending on severity and functional impact.

Hematological Disorders-A group of conditions (e.g., sickle cell disease, leukemia) covered under SSA Listing 7.00 for evaluation of disability.

Hemophilia-A blood clotting disorder considered under SSA Listing 7.08 or evaluated based on frequency and severity of bleeding episodes.

Hepatitis-A liver condition (commonly Hepatitis B or C) that may be considered disabling, especially if it causes severe liver damage or meets Listing 5.05.

Hernia-A medical condition that may be considered disabling if it leads to chronic pain, limited mobility, or complications.

HHS (U.S. Department of Health and Human Services)-The federal agency that oversees public health and administers programs like Medicaid, which interacts with SSA programs.

HIV Infection (Human Immunodeficiency Virus)-Evaluated under SSA Listing 14.11, especially when it causes significant immune suppression or secondary infections.

Hodgkin's Disease (Hodgkin Lymphoma)-A form of cancer evaluated under SSA Listing 13.05.

Homebound Status-A term occasionally relevant in child SSI cases when assessing the impact of a condition on a child's daily functioning and school attendance.

Hospitalization-The frequency and length of hospital stays can be important evidence in demonstrating the severity of an impairment.

Household Income-Relevant in SSI cases, as income from other household members can affect financial eligibility.

Hyperactivity / Hyperkinetic Syndrome-Related to conditions like ADHD, evaluated under the childhood mental disorders listings (112.11).

Hypertension (High Blood Pressure)-While not a listed condition on its own, it is often a contributing factor in other impairments (e.g., heart disease, kidney disease).

Hypothyroidism-A thyroid disorder that may contribute to other impairments but typically must cause functional limitations to be considered disabling.

Hypotonia-A condition of decreased muscle tone, often considered in childhood disability claims (especially with genetic disorders).

I

Impairment-A medically determinable physical or mental condition that limits a person's ability to perform basic work activities.

Impairment-Related Work Expenses (IRWE)-Costs for items or services that a disabled person needs to work, which can be deducted from their income when determining SSI eligibility and payment amounts.

Income- Money received from work, benefits, or other sources. SSA distinguishes between earned income (from work) and unearned income (like gifts, pensions, or other benefits).

Individualized Education Program (IEP)-While primarily related to education, an IEP may be reviewed during child SSI disability claims as evidence of functional limitations.

Initial Determination-The first decision made by SSA on a claim or issue, such as eligibility, benefit amount, or overpayment.

In-kind Support and Maintenance (ISM)-Non-cash assistance, such as food or shelter, received by an SSI applicant or recipient. This can affect the amount of SSI benefits.

Insured Status-The requirement that a person must have worked and paid Social Security taxes for a certain number of quarters to qualify for Social Security Disability Insurance (SSDI).

Intellectual Disability-A condition characterized by significant limitations in intellectual functioning and adaptive behavior. It can be a qualifying condition under SSA's Listing of Impairments.

Intermediate Care Facility-A type of residential care facility that may affect eligibility or payment amounts for SSI recipients.

Intermittent Work History-A sporadic work record that may affect eligibility or the calculation of benefit amounts.

Internal Revenue Service (IRS)-While not part of SSA, the IRS may be involved if backpay or earnings are under review for tax purposes.

J

Job Coach-A person who provides one-on-one support to help individuals with disabilities learn and maintain employment, often part of a supported employment program.

Job Corps-A free education and vocational training program administered by the U.S. Department of Labor that may be referenced in vocational assessments for younger applicants.

Job Description-A detailed account of the duties, responsibilities, and requirements of a particular job; used by SSA when evaluating past relevant work.

Job Duties-Specific tasks an individual performed in past work. SSA uses this to determine whether an applicant can return to past relevant work.

Job Titles-Standardized titles for various occupations used by the Dictionary of Occupational Titles (DOT) or O*NET, referenced in SSA vocational evaluations.

Judgment (Poor Judgment)-A term sometimes used in mental health records or psychological evaluations to describe a symptom that may impact functioning and be considered in a disability determination.

Judicial Review-The process by which a denied Social Security claim can be appealed in federal court after exhausting administrative remedies.

K

Keep Appointment Letter-A notice sent by SSA to remind a claimant of a scheduled consultative examination or other required appointment. Missing this can delay or negatively impact a claim.

Kiddie SSI-Informal term sometimes used to refer to Supplemental Security Income (SSI benefits paid to children under age 18 who meet SSA's definition of disability for minors and who come from low-income households.

Known Impairment-A condition already documented or established in a claimant's medical history that SSA considers during disability determination.

L

Legal Guardian-An individual who has legal authority to make decisions on behalf of another person, often relevant in disability claims involving minors or adults with limited capacity.

Level of Appeal-Refers to the various stages in the disability claim process, such as Reconsideration, Hearing, Appeals Council, and Federal Court.

Licensed Physician-A medical doctor (M.D. or D.O.) who is legally authorized to practice medicine and provide medical evidence in disability claims.

Limitations-Restrictions in a person's ability to perform physical, mental, or sensory activities due to a medical impairment. Limitations are used to assess functional capacity.

Listing of Impairments (Listings)-A medical guide used by SSA to determine if a person's condition is severe enough to qualify for disability benefits without considering age, education, or work experience.

Living Arrangements-The type of housing and household setup a person has, which can affect SSI payment amounts.

Local Social Security Office-A regional SSA office where individuals can apply for benefits, submit documentation, or get assistance with claims

Longitudinal Medical Evidence-Medical records and documentation that cover a period of time and show the progression and treatment of a medical condition.

Low Birth Weight-A specific SSA childhood listing category for infants who are born with a weight below a certain threshold, which may qualify them for disability benefits.

Lump Sum Payment-A one-time payment of past-due disability benefits, often paid when an application is approved after a long wait.

M

Medical Consultant (MC)-A licensed physician who works with SSA to review medical evidence and help determine the severity of a claimant's impairments.

Medical Evidence-Records and documentation from medical sources used to establish the existence and severity of a disability.

Medical Improvement-A reduction in the severity of an impairment. SSA uses this concept to determine if someone still qualifies for disability benefits during continuing disability reviews (CDRs).

Medical Listing-Part of the Listing of Impairments; detailed medical criteria that, if met, automatically qualify an applicant as disabled.

Medically Determinable Impairment (MDI)-A physical or mental condition that is supported by objective medical evidence and can be diagnosed by a licensed medical provider.

Medical Source Statement-A written opinion from a treating provider describing a claimant's functional limitations and how their condition affects their ability to work.

Mental Disorder Listing-A section of the SSA's Listing of Impairments that includes criteria for various mental health conditions like depression, anxiety, and schizophrenia.

Mental Residual Functional Capacity (MRFC)-An assessment of how mental impairments affect a person's ability to perform work-related activities.

Monthly Benefit Amount (MBA)-The amount of money a beneficiary receives each month from Social Security Disability Insurance (SSDI) or Supplemental Security Income (SSI).

My Social Security Account-An online portal provided by SSA that allows users to view their earnings history, benefit estimates, and manage disability claims.

N

Net Earnings from Self-Employment (NESE)-Income that self-employed individuals report to SSA, which is used to determine SSDI eligibility and benefit amounts.

Non-Disability Factors-Eligibility elements unrelated to the disability itself, such as age, marital status, or immigration status.

Non-Exertional Limitation-A restriction that affects a person's ability to work in ways not related to strength, such as difficulty concentrating, anxiety, or inability to follow instructions.

Non-Medical Requirements-Factors unrelated to health that a claimant must meet to qualify for benefits, such as income/resource limits for SSI or work history for SSDI.

Non-Severe Impairment-An impairment that does not significantly limit a person's ability to perform basic work-related activities and therefore does not qualify on its own for disability.

Non-Treating Source-A medical or non-medical source that has not provided regular treatment but may still offer information, such as a one-time consultative examiner.

Notice of Award (NOA)-A formal letter from SSA stating that a claim has been approved and outlining the benefit amount, back pay, and start date.

Notice of Denial-A written notice informing the claimant that their application for benefits has been denied, along with the reasons and appeal rights.

Nurse Practitioner (NP)-An advanced practice registered nurse who can provide medical evidence and opinions in disability cases. SSA recognizes NPs as acceptable medical sources in many cases.

O

Objective Medical Evidence-Evidence obtained from medically acceptable clinical and laboratory diagnostic techniques, such as test results, used to verify a medically determinable impairment (MDI).

Occupational Base-The entire set of jobs a person may be able to do, considering their residual functional capacity (RFC), age, education, and work experience.

Occupational Grid (Medical-Vocational Guidelines)-A set of SSA rules used to determine disability for claimants who can't meet a medical listing but have limitations preventing them from returning to past work.

Office of Appellate Operations (OAO)-The SSA office that processes requests for review filed with the Appeals Council after an ALJ decision.

Office of Hearings Operations (OHO)-The SSA office that schedules and conducts disability hearings before an Administrative Law Judge (ALJ).

Official Disability Guidelines (ODG)-Guidelines sometimes referenced in evaluating disability claims, especially by other entities, though not officially binding on SSA.

Old-Age, Survivors, and Disability Insurance (OASDI)-The formal name for the Social Security program, which includes retirement, survivor, and disability benefits.

Onset Date-The date a claimant alleges or SSA determines their disability began. This date affects eligibility and the amount of back pay.

Overpayment-Benefits paid in excess of what a claimant was legally eligible to receive. SSA may seek repayment of these funds.

Own Occupation-A concept sometimes referenced when evaluating whether a person can return to the specific work they performed before becoming disabled.

P

Partial Disability – A term not typically used in SSA disability, but relevant in workers' comp. SSA uses a total disability standard.

Past Relevant Work (PRW) – Work performed within the last 15 years that was substantial gainful activity (SGA) and lasted long enough for the claimant to learn it. Used to determine whether a claimant can return to their previous work.

Past Work – Work the claimant has performed in the past, usually considered in disability determination for steps 4 and 5 of the sequential evaluation process.
Payee (Representative Payee) – A person or organization appointed by SSA to manage benefits on behalf of someone who cannot manage their own finances.
Period of Disability – A continuous period during which a person is disabled. It can affect eligibility and calculation of benefits.
Physical Residual Functional Capacity (RFC) – An assessment of a person's physical abilities despite impairments, used to determine work capability.
Plan to Achieve Self-Support (PASS) – A program that allows SSI recipients to set aside income or resources to reach a work goal without affecting benefit eligibility.
Prescribed Period – A specific time frame within which an action must be taken, such as the 7-year period after a worker's death for a disabled widow(er) to apply.
Prescribed Treatment – Medical treatment recommended by a treating source. Refusing it without good cause may affect eligibility.
Presumptive Disability – A determination that allows payment of benefits before a final decision is made when the applicant has a condition that clearly meets disability standards (e.g., total blindness, Down syndrome).
Primary Insurance Amount (PIA) – The amount of monthly Social Security benefits a person is entitled to at full retirement age or when disability benefits begin.
Program Operations Manual System (POMS) – SSA's internal manual used by employees to process claims and benefits.
Protective Filing Date – The date a claimant first contacts SSA about filing for benefits. This date can be used as the application date if the formal application is filed within a certain time.
Psychiatric Review Technique (PRT) – A standardized process for evaluating mental impairments in disability claims.

Q

Qualified Alien-A non-citizen who meets specific immigration status requirements under federal law, making them potentially eligible for Supplemental Security Income (SSI).
Quarterly Benefit Estimate-A statement provided by the SSA that gives updated projections of future benefits based on recent earnings and potential retirement or disability scenarios.
Quarters of Coverage (QCs)-Also known as "work credits," these are the units used to determine whether a worker has sufficient work history to qualify for Social Security benefits, including Disability Insurance (SSDI). Typically, a person earns up to four quarters per year based on earnings.
Quick Disability Determination (QDD)-A fast-track SSA process that uses computer-based predictive modeling to identify cases with a high probability of approval and minimal documentation needs, expediting decisions for certain applicants.

R

Reconsideration – The first level of appeal after an initial denial of a Social Security Disability (SSD) or Supplemental Security Income (SSI) claim.
Reevaluation – A periodic review by SSA to determine if a beneficiary still meets the criteria for disability.
Rehabilitation Services – Services such as vocational or medical support aimed at helping a person return to work, sometimes coordinated through SSA's Ticket to Work program.
Representative – An attorney or non-attorney advocate who assists claimants with SSA disability claims and hearings.
Representative Payee – A person or organization appointed by SSA to manage benefits for someone unable to do so themselves.
Residual Functional Capacity (RFC) – An assessment of what a claimant can still do despite their impairments, considering physical and mental limitations.

Resources – Assets considered when determining eligibility for SSI. Limits apply (e.g., $2,000 for individuals, $3,000 for couples).
Retroactive Benefits – Past-due benefits payable for the time between the established onset date of disability and the date of the application (limited to 12 months prior to application for SSDI).
Retroactive Date – The date SSA determines that the disability began for the purposes of calculating back pay.
Review (Continuing Disability Review - CDR) – A scheduled re-examination to verify continued eligibility for disability benefits.
Ruling (Social Security Ruling - SSR) – Official SSA policy interpretations of the law and regulations used in making disability determinations.

S

Scheduled Reexamination – A planned review of a beneficiary's condition to determine continued eligibility.
Schedule of Evaluation – A listing used to determine the severity of impairments based on medical evidence.
Self-Employment Income – Earnings from work done as an independent contractor or business owner; evaluated to determine Substantial Gainful Activity (SGA).
Sequential Evaluation Process – A five-step process SSA uses to determine disability status.
Severe Impairment – A medically determinable impairment that significantly limits physical or mental ability to do basic work activities.
Social Security Administration (SSA) – The federal agency that administers the SSDI and SSI programs.
Social Security Disability Insurance (SSDI) – A benefit program for individuals who are disabled and have sufficient work credits.
Special Senses and Speech – One of SSA's Listing of Impairments categories that includes vision, hearing, and speech disorders.
Spend Down – A process where individuals reduce income/assets to qualify for SSI or Medicaid.
Spinal Disorders – A category of medical impairments under the SSA's listings.
State Disability Determination Services (DDS) – Agencies that make the initial decision on disability claims on behalf of SSA.
Statutory Blindness – A level of visual impairment defined by law that qualifies a person for benefits.
Student Earned Income Exclusion – An SSI work incentive that allows students under 22 to exclude part of their income.
Substantial Gainful Activity (SGA) – A level of work activity and earnings used to determine disability eligibility.
Supplemental Security Income (SSI) – A needs-based program for aged, blind, or disabled individuals with limited income/resources.
Supportive Evidence – Medical or non-medical documentation that supports a disability claim.
Symptom – A claimant's description of physical or mental issues, considered alongside objective evidence.
Systemic Disorders – Impairments that affect multiple body systems, such as lupus or vasculitis.

T

Technical Denial – A denial of a disability claim based on non-medical reasons (e.g., too much income, insufficient work credits), before any medical evaluation is made.
Terminal Illness (TERI) – A case flag for individuals with a medical condition expected to result in death; these cases receive expedited processing.
Third-Party Reporter – Someone other than the claimant who provides SSA with information relevant to a disability determination (e.g., family member, teacher, employer).
Ticket to Work – A voluntary SSA program that helps disability beneficiaries obtain vocational rehabilitation, training, and employment support services.

Timely Filing – Submitting an application, appeal, or form within SSA's prescribed deadlines.
Title II – Refers to the Social Security Disability Insurance (SSDI) program, which provides benefits to disabled individuals who have paid into the Social Security trust fund.
Title XVI – Refers to the Supplemental Security Income (SSI) program, which provides benefits to low-income individuals who are aged, blind, or disabled.
Total Disability – The SSA standard requiring that a person be unable to perform any substantial gainful activity due to medically determinable impairments lasting at least 12 months or expected to result in death.
Transmittal Sheet – A form used in disability cases to summarize and transmit key information from one SSA component or level to another (e.g., from DDS to the hearing office).
Treating Source – A medical professional who has provided the claimant with medical treatment or evaluation and has an ongoing treatment relationship.
Trial Work Period (TWP) – A work incentive that allows SSDI recipients to test their ability to work for up to nine months without losing benefits, regardless of earnings.

U

Under Review-The status indicating that a claim or continuing disability review (CDR) is currently being evaluated by SSA.
Unearned Income-Income not earned through work, such as child support, interest, pensions, or gifts. It can affect SSI eligibility and benefit amounts.
Unfavorable Decision-A denial issued by an Administrative Law Judge (ALJ) after a hearing. This means the claimant was found not disabled.
Unskilled Work-Work that requires little or no judgment and can be learned in a short time (generally 30 days or less). SSA uses this classification in determining residual functional capacity (RFC).
Unstated Impairment-A condition or symptom not explicitly claimed by the applicant but discovered during review or examination that may affect the disability finding.
Unsuccessful Work Attempt (UWA)-A period of work that is stopped or reduced below the SGA level due to the claimant's disability within six months of starting. It may not count against the claimant when determining eligibility.
Updated Medical Evidence-New medical records submitted during a claim or appeal that SSA must consider when determining disability.
Urgent Case Processing-Special handling of certain disability claims due to critical need, such as terminal illness (TERI), military casualty, or dire need.

V

Vaccine Injury – A medical condition resulting from a vaccine that may potentially be considered in SSA disability claims if it causes lasting impairment.
Valid IQ Score – A clinically administered IQ score used in evaluating intellectual disorders under SSA listings (e.g., Listing 12.05).
Variable Income – Income that fluctuates; may impact SSA determinations of Substantial Gainful Activity (SGA).
Verification – The process SSA uses to confirm information (such as income, medical records, employment history) relevant to disability claims.
Vestibular Disorders – Medical conditions affecting balance and spatial orientation; may be evaluated under SSA Listing 2.07.
Veterans Affairs-(VA) – The U.S. Department of Veterans Affairs; SSA may coordinate benefits with the VA if a claimant receives both VA and SSA disability benefits.
Vocational Adjustment – SSA considers whether a claimant can adapt to other work based on age, education, and work experience.
Vocational Assessment – Evaluation conducted to determine a claimant's ability to work or retrain for other employment.

Vocational Background – The claimant's prior work history, job skills, and training, which are considered when assessing ability to work.
Vocational Consultant – An expert who may testify at a hearing regarding a claimant's ability to perform past or other work.
Vocational Evidence – Information such as job descriptions, skill levels, and labor market data used to assess work capability.
Vocational Expert (VE) – A professional called during SSA hearings to offer testimony about the claimant's ability to work given their impairments.
Vocational Factor(s) – Factors like age, education, work experience, and skill level considered when determining disability under the medical-vocational guidelines (grid rules).
Vocational Guidelines (Grid Rules) – SSA's medical-vocational framework used to determine disability status for claimants with non-exertional limitations.
Vocational Rehabilitation-(VR) – Services aimed at helping individuals with disabilities return to work. SSA may support VR programs and offer incentive programs like the Ticket to Work.
Voluntary Cessation of Work – When a claimant chooses to stop working, SSA assesses whether it was due to disability or other factors.

W

Wage Earner-The individual whose work record is used to determine eligibility for Social Security benefits, including SSDI.
Wages-Compensation for employment, which includes salaries, commissions, bonuses, and other forms of earned income. Wages are considered in determining SSI eligibility and SSDI work activity.
Waiting Period-A mandatory five-month period after the onset of disability during which no SSDI benefits are paid. It does not apply to SSI.
Waiver-A formal decision by SSA not to collect an overpayment from a beneficiary, usually due to financial hardship or lack of fault.
Work Activity-Any work performed by a claimant that SSA evaluates to determine whether the work is Substantial Gainful Activity (SGA).
Work Credits-Also called quarters of coverage, these are earned by working and paying Social Security taxes. A certain number are required for SSDI eligibility.
Worker's Compensation Offset-If a disabled worker receives both SSDI and workers' compensation, SSA may reduce SSDI to ensure combined benefits don't exceed a certain threshold.
Workforce Innovation and Opportunity Act (WIOA)-Federal law intended to improve access to employment, education, and training, especially for individuals with disabilities.
Work History Report (Form SSA-3369)-A detailed form used in disability evaluations to document a claimant's job history for the past 15 years.
Work Incentives-SSA programs (such as Trial Work Period and Ticket to Work) that allow beneficiaries to test their ability to work without immediately losing benefits.
Working While Disabled-SSA allows limited work activity under certain programs while still receiving disability benefits, especially during the Trial Work Period.
Work Review-SSA's periodic evaluation of a beneficiary's earnings and activities to determine continued eligibility for disability benefits.

X

X-Chromosome-One of the two sex chromosomes. Disorders linked to the X-chromosome (such as Fragile X syndrome) can result in developmental and intellectual disabilities.
Xenobiotic-A chemical compound foreign to a living organism. Some xenobiotics may cause toxic exposures leading to disability, especially in occupational environments.
Xeroderma Pigmentosum (XP)-A rare genetic disorder characterized by extreme sensitivity to ultraviolet rays, leading to skin and eye abnormalities. It can be disabling due to the required life-long sun protection and increased cancer risk.

Xerostomia-Also known as dry mouth, it can result from certain medications or medical conditions like Sjögren's syndrome. In severe cases, it may contribute to disability if it affects nutrition or speech.
X-Linked Disorder-A genetic condition caused by mutations on the X chromosome. These can include conditions like Duchenne muscular dystrophy or Rett syndrome, which may be relevant in disability evaluations.
X-Ray-A diagnostic imaging technique used to evaluate physical impairments, injuries, or internal medical conditions relevant to disability claims.

Y

Yearly Earnings Test-A rule under Social Security Retirement, but relevant for SSDI beneficiaries returning to work. If earnings exceed a certain annual amount, benefits may be reduced.
Year of Onset-Refers to the calendar year when a claimant's disability began, as established by medical and other evidence.
Younger Individual (Age 18–49)-SSA considers individuals aged 18–49 as "younger individuals" in the medical-vocational guidelines (the grid rules), which influences disability determinations based on age, education, and work history.
Your Earnings Record-The personal work and earnings history used by SSA to calculate benefits eligibility and payment amounts for SSDI.
Youth with Disabilities-Refers to individuals under age 22 who may qualify for Childhood Disability Benefits (CDB) if they have a qualifying disability that began before age 22 and have a parent receiving retirement, disability, or deceased benefits.

Z

Z Codes (ICD-10-CM)-Diagnostic codes from the *International Classification of Diseases, 10th Revision, Clinical Modification* used to capture reasons for encounters other than a disease or injury (e.g., social determinants of health).
Zero Net Benefit-A situation where the SSDI or SSI benefit is entirely offset by other income (e.g., workers' compensation or pensions).
Zero-Rated Work Activity-Work that is evaluated as having no substantial gainful activity (SGA) value due to minimal earnings or minimal duties.
Zone Program Integrity Contractor (ZPIC)-Contractors used by CMS (Centers for Medicare & Medicaid Services) to identify and investigate potential fraud, waste, or abuse in Medicare services.

A

B

C

www.ingramcontent.com/pod-product-compliance
Lightning Source LLC
LaVergne TN
LVHW081947200926
848484LV00009B/2520